THE
FRUITFUL
Retirement

A FINANCIAL GUIDE
FOR YOUR LIFE'S GREATEST CHAPTER

JIM DEGAETANO, CPA, CFP®

The Fruitful Retirement
A Financial Framework for Your Life's Greatest Chapter
By Jim DeGaetano

Published by Tremendous Leadership
PO Box 267
Boiling Springs, PA 17007
717-701-8159
www.TremendousLeadership.com

The author and publisher assume no responsibilities for errors or omissions or for damages resulting from the use of the information contained herein. The information contained in this publication is intended solely to provide general guidance on matters of interest for the personal use of the reader. Laws, regulations, and practice change constantly and vary throughout the world. As such, this book is not meant to provide individual, personal, or professional tax, legal, or other professional advice. All professionals are responsible for adhering to the rules, regulations, and laws of their companies and jurisdiction where they practice. It is recommended and expected for the reader to work with a reputable financial advisor for applying all matters discussed within.

First Edition

Printed in the United States of America.

Hardcover ISBN 978-1-949033-41-0
Paperback ISBN 978-1-949033-42-7
Ebook ISBN 978-1-949033-43-4

Securities and advisory serviced offered through LPL Financial, a registered investment advisor. Member FINRA/SIPC (A/O 10/01/2020)

ENDORSEMENTS

"What struck me about The Fruitful Retirement is that it's as much about living your best life as it is about planning for retirement. Most people think about life after work through a purely financial lens, but Jim DeGaetano takes a bigger and better approach, which is to talk to his clients first about the emotional aspects. By first personalizing and defining what retirement means for YOU, Jim can then help craft a practical financial plan to achieve that vision. I highly recommend this book for anyone looking to make their retirement dreams a reality."

–Dan Arnold, CEO, LPL Financial

"Retirement itself is not the magical destination society tells us it is, but you can choose to make it magical. The Fruitful Retirement is a powerful tool to help you think about the endless possibilities for the next chapter of your life and how you can be prepared for them."

–Tara Bradford, Host of Handle Everything Podcast

"I don't understand financial matters!", "Having Money is a mystery!", and "When I get some extra money I'll get a plan!" are all myths or lies we use to deceive ourselves which only results in compounding our problems. Jim DeGaetano opens our eyes regardless of our age, status, or compensation. A few hours spent with "The Fruitful Retirement" will once again prove the age-old adage: "You don't get the money to get the plan, you get the plan to get the money!" Simply put, Jim wants everyone to know if you have desires, discipline, and determination

you too can have "A Fruitful Retirement". A quick, entertaining, and thoughtful read with a purpose!
–Mike Wheeler, Former National Director/Executive
Vice President, First Command Financial Services

"Thoughtfully written. Timely, practical and valuable."
–Gary Holland, CEO, Charter Financial Planning
Network, Financial Advisor Magazine

"Jim DeGaetano has written a retirement planning masterpiece. His thought-provoking questions and exercises hit the mark and are surpassed only by the extensive wisdom that he shares. The Fruitful Retirement is a practical, powerful guide for anyone looking to maximize their wealth, security, and satisfaction in retirement."
–Dr. Rick Jensen, Performance Coach, Sport
Psychologist, & Author

ACKNOWLEDGMENTS

I am blessed to have a wonderful wife that loves me for who I am and supports my life's work. At times it means long hours and the occasional change of plans for dinner. I once read a quote by Jack Nicklaus stating that he was great at hitting a little white ball because his wife was so good at everything else. Well, I'm horrible at golf, but would like to think that I've been able to focus my energy on creating fruitful retirements for my clients because of my wife's attention to everything else, most importantly our beautiful two children. For this I could not be more grateful.

There is no branch that bears fruit by itself. I have been very fortunate to have supportive parents who have always provided a framework in life to learn. They raised me to give my best, and that hard work yields dividends in the future. I'm grateful for their love and I hope to 'pay it forward' to my own children. They provided me three wonderful sisters that encouraged me along the way and whether they realize it or not, gave me an education on the softer side of communication. I learned that true empathy comes from engaged listening. Words matter and can have a lasting impact. In fact, it is the reason I wrote this book.

When I came up with the concept of The Fruitful Retirement years ago, I knew that it would become a focal point for my business and that the concept was something that could be adapted by other advisors. The thought of a book took a back seat when I started my firm in 2017. It was not until two years later when I joined a peer coaching program with other great financial advisors across the Country that the idea was revived. My wonderful colleagues gave me inspiration to finish the book. Fellow advisor author Jonathan Bednar was very helpful as I started navigating the process. Our amazing coach Dr. Rick Jensen provided valuable insight that saved time and energy, and even threw in a few golf tips during a session. Many thanks to my team at the office, starting with my wonderful office manager Rebecca Brennan-Meyer who took the liberty to start scheduling bi-weekly Fridays at the local Bosler library for me to put pen to paper. My colleague and great advisor Christina Ward graciously took time out of her day to bring clarity to particular topics and I cannot forget to mention Joe Elwood, who has been very supportive during this whole process. The process took well over a year after finally scheduling time at the library.

Publishing a book has many facets, from the editorial to marketing to legal and whether to self-publish. After beginning the process, I was introduced to Candice Elliott in New Orleans from 'Listen Money Matters' to help with the first part of the editorial process and she got me started on the right path. Much gratitude goes to Tara Bradford of Rae Media Group for her efforts to keep me focused in the right direction, creating our website, and helping me to become 'social media acceptable' to the world. She is a creative genius. I appreciate Tom Yates from Advisor Assist LLC and Kelley Keller of the Keller Law firm for their attention in keeping me legally compliant. I also must acknowledge LPL Financial for their support along the way. Rob Holmes, Tim Halbig, and Kevin Pollard - you are appreciated. Chris Maraist was also a believer in me from the beginning, and many thanks for his insurance support.

The decision to self-publish or hire a publisher is one filled with many questions for a first-time author. I greatly appreciated the time spent with the folks at Advantage|Forbes Books during the visioning process. I eventually decided that relying on the expertise of a hybrid publisher was the best fit for this book and that decision was reinforced after I met Tracey Jones with Tremendous Leadership. Mike Wheeler's thoughts after the first draft were invaluable and kept me going. Shane Thompson's editorial capacity, coupled with Leah Hess's graphical abilities were "tremendous" as advertised throughout the process. My gratitude is tremendous.

My life has been full of wonderful mentors too numerous to mention. Some of you know who you are, while a good many may not realize the training that I have received by listening to your words and observing your actions. I am truly blessed to have amazing clients that are like family to me. This book could not have been written without all of you, and I truly thank you for your encouragement, support, wisdom, and love over the years.

*Dedicated to my parents
Jim Sr. and Barb DeGaetano.
May you enjoy a Fruitful Retirement. You deserve it!*

TABLE OF CONTENTS

PROLOGUE

I commend you for making the decision to read this book. You, dear reader, are a minority in this world. You have made the decision to take control of your future. Sadly, many people are not able to live independently and have the kind of fulfilling retirement that most of us dream of—one in which we don't have to worry about finances and instead are able to pursue our goals and hobbies.

That you've purchased this book signals to me that you are motivated to create a successful retirement plan and that you understand the blueprints are already out there. We are not reinventing the wheel, as many have come before you that navigated the path that you are about to follow.

It is true that there is no such thing as a one-size-fits-all retirement plan. That's what The Fruitful Retirement is all about.

This is not your typical retirement book. There are already thousands of books out there that talk about the financial issues around retirement, how to prepare for it, how to accumulate money for it, how to spend money during it. I talk to a lot of clients about their fears around retirement and, by a wide margin, the one I hear most often is "I'm afraid to run out of money."

So, while we are going to talk about financial issues, we're also going to talk about something else that is just as important as your money: YOUR LIFE. Namely, what are you going to do with the rest of it?

It's a scary question. You probably haven't been in this position since you were a kid when well-meaning adults asked what you wanted to be when you grew up. And you're in a similar position now, with many years ahead of you and endless possibilities—which is why it is so scary. You can do whatever you want, but what if you don't know what you want?!

This is a common fear. Usually, this feeling subsides after we have discussed your plans and a wave of relief washes over you. You can see that through your effort and planning you can visualize the path of a secure retirement. You let out a deep breath and ask, "What next?"

In the beginning of my career, I didn't really have an answer, but because I heard the question so often, phrased in a variety of ways, I decided to find an answer for my clients—well, help them find their own answers. This book is the culmination of many years of learning, not just in the classroom, but more importantly, listening to my clients, family, friends, mentors, and the issues they faced when entering their greatest chapter in life.

The Fruitful Retirement walks you through the process of obtaining clarity, both emotionally and financially, for a successful transition into the chapter of your life after employment. I will talk about finding the emotional clarity in the first part of the book and will include some exercises to help you answer that question for yourself. The second part will provide the framework for your financial clarity, and in the final part I will offer some thoughts about your overall retirement plan.

Welcome to the rest of your life and a Fruitful Retirement!

Part I

The Art of Being Fruitful

*Being fruitful is about a lot more than accumulating money and possessions; the art of being fruitful is about **creating the kind of life you want to live.***

I love to work out and stay in shape. Over the years I have read many articles on ways to keep fit and have noticed that all workouts are not the same. We all have different sizes, shapes, and stresses in our lives that require different strategies to improving our physical and mental health.

In fact, there are three general categories of body types for men and women: ectomorph, mesomorph, and endomorph. Each of these describes how our bodies are shaped, how they respond to food, and how our hormonal and sympathetic nervous systems react to our environments. Collectively, these variables affect our metabolic response to nutrition and training.

Similarly, I have observed over many years of consulting in many thousands of retirement planning discussions that families entering retirement fall into one of three categories much the same way we fall into one of three body types. Our wealth profiles have different shapes and sizes, we "metabolize" risk and the anxiety of change at different rates, and we each have our own biases and behaviors that may result in blind spots in our planning— all of which testifies to the benefits of adopting a retirement income-planning process tailored to our particular constitutions.

It seems to me, then, that we might approach our fiscal fitness the same way we approach our physical fitness, first by identifying our dominant body type—or wealth profile—and then by designing an appropriate diet and workout regimen—or retirement plan—to maximize our health and wealth. The prevailing metaphor of this model relates our various wealth profiles to fruit.

Yes, fruit.

Each piece of fruit represents a type of retirement situation with its associated strategy to mitigate its inherent risks. Once you know which fruit you are, you can customize retirement plan that best suits your Needs. And it's simpler than you imagine.

In the world of personal finance and retirement planning, the amount of information out there can be overwhelming. The media would have us believe that in order to be a successful investor, we must watch, read, and listen to finance-related content every day and, if we don't, we will be caught unaware when the next bubble bursts and wipes out our life savings.

My email inbox is flooded with get-rich-quick schemes and, conversely, warnings about the next disaster to strike. When someone is trying to scare you, chances are pretty good that they have a monetary stake in doing so. Keep that in mind whenever you see or hear an *Oh my gosh, the sky is falling!* financial headline.

I could go on, but you get the point. All of this can be stressful and cause you to second guess yourself. Five, ten, or twenty years ago, you thought your retirement savings were on schedule. Now that retirement has become a less faraway concept and more of your soon-to-be reality, doubt can set in and make you vulnerable to basing financial decisions on fear rather than an objective strategy.

Of all the many books written on this topic, this one is unique in at least two ways: first, it infuses the qualitative and quantitative aspects of preparing for retirement; and, second, it allows you to visualize your retirement planning based on which type of fruit best represents your *current situation.*

This book is designed to provide a simple framework to help anyone who plans to stop getting a paycheck from their employer at some point in their life. It is NOT meant to be a substitute for working with a trustworthy financial advisor who can guide you during each stage of life.

Chapter 1

The Rationality of Retirement

Humans are not rational beings. Making good financial decisions is a lot like making good dietary decisions. We all know that eating broccoli is healthier than eating chocolate cake, but knowing the right thing and doing it are two different things. Sometimes we choose the cake. Personally, if the menu has peanut butter as part of any dessert, I can't say no.

This is why a good financial advisor is also something of a good psychiatrist. There is an entire subset of economics called behavioral economics that focuses on how humans make decisions related to our finances. It responds to the assumption that people are rational creatures and acknowledges that, as in many other areas of life, people's financial decisions are influenced more by emotions than they would like to admit.

Any financial advisor worth their salt understands this and can spot it in clients, explain it to them (without being condescending), and put plans in place to help them make the best decision when fear or panic try to lead them in the wrong direction.

A good financial advisor is also a good mediator or even a marriage counselor. The ideal financial marriage is made up of a saver and a spender, but this combination can lead to disagreements between spouses. The saver sometimes thinks their partner is extravagant, sure to drive them both into the poor house, while the spender sometimes thinks the other is stingy and too frugal, determined to take the fun out of life.

An advisor can show this kind of couple that there is a middle ground, a place where both partners might not be totally happy with spending decisions but neither is angry or resentful.

I probably don't have to tell you that financial issues are one of the leading causes of marital arguments and divorce. When you are a committee of two, there is no majority. So, sometimes, a good financial advisor functions as a tiebreaker. If two partners cannot agree on a major financial decision, their advisor can act as a mediator. From where I stand, money would not be a leading cause of divorce if there were a solid plan in place that has been mutually determined and accepted.

As you near retirement, you and your partner may have been married for decades. You may not need to say a lot because you know what the other is going to say before they say it. However, it is important to discuss financial issues as often as you did earlier in your relationship to keep the two of you on the same page. Please note that doesn't necessarily mean you have the same vision of how to spend your money but that you are aware of each other's vision and have a plan that satisfies you both. You should discuss money openly to allow for any fears to surface, especially considering all the changes that come with retirement.

It is not uncommon for one partner to handle all the household finances. Any number of reasons might account for this: one is better with money and one enjoys handling finances, while one hates dealing with money. It is very important that the partner not handling the finances have an understanding, at least at a basic level, of the financial situation.

What happens when the partner who always deals with the finances dies or becomes incapacitated? This is a team sport, and both partners should have a relationship with all the other members of the team, such as the financial advisor, tax professional, lawyer, and insurance agent, to name a few.

Would you send your partner to your annual health exam or dental checkup? Well, I'm sure you would love to, but there is no way for the doctor to review *your* physical or dental health if you are not there. The same can be said for planning for your retirement; both spouses should be involved.

If you and your spouse do not handle the finances together, that needs to change. It doesn't have to be 50/50, but you both need to know how much money is coming in, going out, and where it is going each month; how much money you have saved; how the money will be disbursed and replenished; where all of your financial accounts and other relevant documents (life insurance policies, estate documents, etc.) are and how to access them; and so on.

If you are single, divorced, or widowed, there may also be other people in your life at the moment that are affected by your retirement. What if you happen to become mentally incapable of handling your finances or die prematurely? You are not alone and while it may not be a partner, taking a moment to think about who in your life you may want to 'bring onto the team' to know your plan and the other professionals on your team is important.

This book can be a great supplement to the work you are already doing with your financial team or a guide to help you begin the process. As a financial advisor who has had thousands of one-on-one appointments with clients, I have designed this book to bring a different perspective to the topic of retirement.

By the time you finish this book, my goal is to help you be better aware of your situation, a choice of strategies to employ in pursuit of your goals, knowledge of the risks that could derail your plan, and the tools you need to mitigate risks.

You will completely understand how a piece of fruit can represent your retirement, which fruit represents your retirement and, consequently, be better able to deploy a strategy based on your type of fruit. Before we get there, however, we need to start at the beginning and discuss why money is so important to us.

So, let's start the journey.

Chapter 2

The Stages of Retirement

*Life is in different stages. Every stage of life is
the foundation for the next stage of life.*

– Lailah Gifty

I devote much of the first part of this book to exploring the emotional aspects of retirement because of their importance to having a happy, healthy, and successful future. At the end of this chapter, you will find exercises to help you plan your time during this new phase of life.

You have likely heard of the stages of grief and loss. Depending on the model you are familiar with, there can be five or seven stages, and they may occur in any order. The stages are:

- Shock: Initial paralysis at hearing the bad news
- Denial: Trying to avoid the inevitable
- Anger: Frustrated outpouring of bottled-up emotion
- Bargaining: Seeking in vain for a way out
- Depression: Final realization of the inevitable
- Testing: Seeking realistic solutions
- Acceptance: Finally finding the way forward

The value of such a model is to help us locate ourselves on a difficult and disorienting landscape following a life crisis. Now, while retirement is not a crisis per se, it may very well be experienced as a loss. And loss can plunge us into an emotional whirlpool. So many years working with people nearing and in retirement have shown me that nearly all of them go through at least four distinct stages of transition:

- Acknowledgment
- Anxiety
- Action
- Acceptance

Acknowledgment

This is the point at which you start contemplating retirement, considering it, kicking around the idea of what it might look like. Maybe you talk about it with your spouse or a few friends who are nearing retirement age themselves. Or talking to some friends who have already retired to pick their brains about what it has been like for them.

Retirement at this stage is still a far-off concept, so while you are thinking about it, you don't yet feel strong emotions about it. Now is the best time to start thinking about how you will spend your time when a third (or more!) of your day is no longer spent working. You have spent decades planning for retirement insofar as you have saved and invested money for it, but you have likely given little thought to how you will fill your time.

Anxiety

Now is when you start to feel like this retirement thing this could be real; there will be a time when you no longer go to work every day and it is not far off. You probably have a lot of questions racing through your mind:

Should I do this? Can I do this? Do I have enough money to do this? If not, what does that mean? What if I die?

When should I start taking Social Security? How does Medicare work and how will I pay for healthcare? What if my spouse or I have a major health event? What if one of us dies early in retirement? How do my assets transfer? Which accounts should I use first, and how does that work? Will taxes take a lot out of my retirement? What if my parents need my financial help to pay for long-term care? Should I stay in my home or move? How do I leave a Legacy for my kids or grandkids and still be okay for retirement?

When this begins to happen, our behavioral biases tend to kick in. We all have certain negative tendencies, but our brains can adapt to new patterns of thought. One of the more widely known negative biases is loss aversion, which is where people essentially feel the pain of loss greater than the pleasure of gain. The statistics on this suggest a ratio of 2:1, meaning you feel the loss twice as much as the gain.

When retirement is twenty years away, you may have been okay staying the course during a recession and market drop, but now that you are in the red zone and looking to retire soon, you view it much differently. Potential retirees will tell me they cannot handle market drops because they do not have the time to recover. I respond by asking whether their doctor has given them a date of death that I should be aware of, since they look quite healthy and ready for a multi-decade retirement filled with fun and happiness.

If you do not think you "suffer from" loss aversion, ask yourself this: Would you rather have a portfolio that could potentially gain 10% or lose 5% in any given year or a portfolio that has the potential to gain 5% with no loss. If your first instinct was the latter, you are loss averse. It is important to note that it is okay to be concerned about your money. This is common, and frankly, you would be in the minority if you did not have any worries. You certainly would not be reading this book.

All your concerns and worries, some real and some imagined, come up during the anxiety stage. Being able to answer these questions is why having a retirement income plan is vital. Now is the time to consider hiring a financial professional who is an expert in dealing with the distribution of your monies if you do not currently work with one. If you are already working with a professional, it is time to talk about your intent to retire soon.

But keep in mind that not all advisors have the same specialty. One who was very skilled at helping you to create a plan that allowed you to accumulate enough wealth in the past may not be an expert at the distribution phase. You only get one chance to do this right, and the stakes are very high. So, whether you are evaluating your current advisor or searching for a new one, ask a lot of questions about their process.

A skilled retirement planner will have expert knowledge in areas like Social Security, pensions, taxation on retirement income, annuities, health insurance and health care options, and the pros and cons of different withdrawal methods.

More precisely, you want someone who can give you advice specific to your circumstances around the following:

- When to start taking Social Security and what kind of spousal or survivor benefits you should apply for
- What your pension distribution options are, the best age to begin, whether you should take them as a lump sum or annuity, and the best survivor option to select

- Your options for withdrawal strategies
- Tax-reduction strategies
- Strategies to protect your income from a big downturn in the market
- How to deal with the impact inflation will have on your spending power
- Long-term care insurance
- What Medicare does and does not pay for and how to close the gap

You will find at the end of this book a list of designations that potential financial planners may possess. I will explain what each one means and the areas of competence that the qualifying exams focus on. For example, a CFP®, issued by the Certified Financial Planner Board of Standards, represents a standard of excellence for financial planners, whether the planners are competent in the areas of financial planning, tax insurance, estate planning, retirement planning, and ethics in financial planning.

Hiring the right advisor can go a long way in easing the anxieties you are dealing with as you get closer to retirement and can give you the confidence to move forward. That said, some of you may be reading this book because you want to do it yourself. Should that be the case, you will still need to develop a plan to address all the concerns listed above as well as assemble a team to execute that plan.

Action

Right now, you are very serious about your desire to stop working. You go to work every day thinking, *I'm really ready. I can see myself not being here anymore.* That doesn't mean you are free of anxiety; you know you need to get a clear vision of your financial reality. The intention now becomes a near-term goal, not something that you've seen as a distant goal over the years.

The first step is to find the appropriate professional, one you feel comfortable with, who has a process that focuses on the distribution of your money, and who understands taxes and the complexities of the next 30 years of your life.

The next step is to create a retirement budget. I have lost count of the number of times that my clients getting close to retirement have told me that this is one of the most helpful, anxiety-reducing exercises they ever do. Seeing on paper (or on the computer screen) how much money will be coming in and how they will be spending it answers a lot of the questions that have been buzzing around in their heads since the acknowledgment stage.

I have included a budget that will work for you, and I will walk you through it. It will allow you to determine which of the three categories—which fruit—you fit into. Once you know where you fall, you can move forward and create your retirement income plan.

Acceptance

The fourth and final phase is acceptance. This is the phase that gives me the most satisfaction as I work with clients. You have gone through the first three phases. Now you have a plan of action that has quelled your anxieties. I have shared tears of joy with many clients when they truly comprehended that they can retire with confidence.

Your retirement income plan should include flexibility for the what-if factors during the next few decades, such as premature death, unforeseen healthcare situations or family events, another great recession, tax or estate law changes, spending flexibility, and a change in the way you want to pass on your legacy.

One of the biggest lessons I learned early on in my career was that we are far better off when we focus on what we can control and accept the things we cannot. It is at this stage of acceptance that you have come to accept this truth and realize that in the short term market fluctuations and economic cycles come and go regardless of how you wake up in the morning—just as taxes will shift with the ever-changing winds of political expediency.

The acceptance phase is a long one. Actually, accepting that you have enough money to live a Fruitful Retirement can be accomplished relatively quickly. But there are a few emotional stages involved in the acceptance phase that have nothing to do with money or taxes or estate planning, and they can take longer to traverse.

Immediately after retirement, you will have that feeling that you had as a kid when the final bell rang on the last day of school before summer vacation. *Freedom!* That is what retirement will feel like—at first—and for some people, for a long time. Maybe the whole time.

You're giddy at the thought of all the possibilities. You can travel, move to a new place, sleep as late as you want, spend more time on your hobbies, take two hours every morning to read the paper and drink your coffee. The world is your oyster. How long this feeling lasts will depend on how much time you have spent prior to the big moment envisioning exactly what you would do to fill your time. It is important.

If you haven't given much thought to what you will do, you might find that the giddiness doesn't last all that long. Maybe you had a list of things you wanted to do during retirement, but they were more like making a list of things you want to do on vacation than creating a new life. Once you have exhausted your list, maybe even done everything twice, you will start to think, *Is this it?*

Even for those who do have a plan to fill their days, getting into a routine or a rhythm can take time. We have spent decades being on someone else's time schedule, so it can be tough to create a schedule for ourselves. A lot of new retirees tend to stick to the hours of their old work life: getting up, eating meals, and going to bed at the same time. I find this is especially true for the clients I work with who have retired from the military. Many jobs have a set schedule, but few are as regimented as the military.

There is certainly nothing wrong with sticking to your old schedule; having a sort of built-in time template can be helpful. Just make sure it's the best template for you.

I will circle back to the concept of acceptance at the end of the book.

Chapter 3

Living an Abundant Life

Love is a fruit in season at all times,
and within reach of every hand.

– Mother Teresa

Abundance is described in the Merriam-Webster Dictionary as "a large amount of something." But, if I asked a group of individuals for their own definition, I would get different answers from each person. This is because the *something* in the dictionary definition means something different to everyone. It is subjective based on our level of consciousness.

I believe that before you map out a path for the future, you must understand where you are right now.

For the purpose of this book, that future is the ever-changing, often misunderstood, sometimes too-distant concept called retirement. To enjoy abundance later in life, we must first understand where it comes from and how we gather it.

Why would I be writing to you about this, you might ask. Is this not a retirement book? Well, yes, kind of! I know you bought this book to help you achieve a Fruitful Retirement, but as you now see, **a Fruitful Retirement is not built on the number of dollars you have in the bank alone.**

There are many self-help books in circulation today, and they will suggest that the path to living a happy life is to focus on finding your purpose. Many of these books become bestsellers because this topic is intrinsically important to all of us. In fact, the most widely read book of all time, the Bible, is a personal roadmap to the path of living your life on purpose.

So, yes, this is a self-help book about money, but before we get to the part that deals with the finances, we need to ascertain what it is we truly want in life.

Whether or not you are religious, spiritual, or disbelieve in a higher power is not the purpose of this book. From my perspective, we are all connected in this world and should treat each other with respect and without judgement. We are all brothers and sisters born with the 'forgotten song' in our soul that needs to be awakened during this journey. Our birth starts with the blindness of not truly being able to see. We spend our whole lives learning, experiencing the good and bad, and many times focusing on our bodies instead of our mind and soul. We attempt to use our past to guide us to change and find true peace in our life. Our vision is distorted by our circumstances that we feel represent our true reality, when in effect, letting go and giving ourselves to something greater than us is where true vision rests. This is the reality where we find happiness and peace. There are a few tangible guarantees in life. One is taxes, and the other is that our hearts have a finite number of beats. However, there are also a few intangible guarantees in life as well, one of which is that the more you awaken within yourself the more abundance the world reveals to you. Why waste any more of those heartbeats on activities that do not bring us into alignment with what would bring us the blessings of abundance? There is a saying that to move forward, one should 'forgive and forget'. I suggest taking this a step further to 'forgive and surrender'. Letting go of any preconceived notions of what you are expected to do in retirement and embracing your spirit for what it was meant to be will make all the difference. It has been said that love is the water of life. This is your chance to turn on the spigot if you have yet to do so. If you are excited about this, you should be! I'm excited with you! For this book to provide the utmost clarity for you and your financial situation, we must start with the direct question of finding what is truly important to you and how you define abundance.

I will go out on a limb and state that the majority of readers will not list money as their number one priority. While money is a necessary part of life, it is merely a tool that allows us to do what we want, provided we have the time. Financial independence means we have the time to focus on the activities that bring joy and peace to our lives. Joy is experiencing happiness independent of our circumstances.

The purpose of this book is to focus on creating and living the Fruitful life, and the ability to adopt solid financial habits early in life goes a long way toward the creation of wealth and freedom. This allows the ability to spend your time and energy living out your reason for being in this world. Designing your Fruitful Retirement is a blend of art and math, fused together to create a purpose in your life that is financially sustainable.

Financial independence means we have the time to focus on the activities that bring joy and peace to our lives.

While making money is part of the financial independence equation, our attitudes and behaviors around it are more important than how much we make.

Your Financial Garden

The condition of the soil in which we sow seeds determines whether the things we plant flourish and bear fruit or wither on the vine. Fertile soil supports healthy plant growth by nourishing their root systems, providing oxygen, nutrients, and water. When we plant a seed in good soil and tend it properly over time, it yields abundance. None of this happens in a vacuum. A branch does not bear fruit alone. You cannot chuck a seed into a hole, walk away, and come back weeks later expecting to find a fruitful plant.

Our finances are the same. We have to start with healthy soil (knowledge) and tend our plant regularly (budgeting, saving, investing, etc.). As the seasons change, how we care for our plant changes too, but we are always tending, always mindful. In return, this mindful awareness allows our money to grow and provide an abundant life and a Fruitful Retirement.

Redefining Retirement

While we will use the term *retirement* in this book, I have never been a fan of the word because the word *retire* means to cease or stop from an activity. I prefer the phrase *financial independence* because it denotes freedom from outside control or support.

Financial independence simply means you no longer have to work solely in order to bring in an income. Your income is derived from other sources. And isn't this what we truly want? The freedom to do what we want and how we want is the ultimate in life flexibility.

We must redefine retirement for the world we live in now, which is very different from the world of our parents and grandparents. Not so long ago, people retired in their 60s, they retired with a pension, and they didn't live as long as we do now. But things don't look like that anymore.

Some people want to retire early—*really early*—in their 30s and 40s. Most of us no longer work for employers that offer pension plans, and we live into our 80s and beyond. In fact, according to recent actuary figures, a non-smoking couple aged 65 has a 25% chance that one of them will be living well into their 90s.

So, the old picture we have of retirement, a grey-haired old couple sitting on their porch in rocking chairs and maybe playing golf once a week, is no longer relevant. Thirty or forty or even fifty years is a lot of time to fill up with chair-rocking and golf.

And guess what? You get to redefine retirement however you want. You have a blank canvas. Now, a blank canvas can be intimidating, so I have placed some exercises at the end of this chapter to help you fill that canvas in.

Many people want to continue to work in some capacity during retirement, and employers are happy to have them. No company wants to lose senior-level, skilled employees, so working into a phased-in retirement has become a popular option. The beauty of this phased approach is both the employer and employee have time to adjust to the change. Going from full time to half time to quarter time can ease the transition for you and your company.

Another approach is to do something totally different, something you just enjoy doing and doing it part time. If you have planned appropriately and are financially secure, earning money is not important. So, how much you're making isn't the primary consideration.

I remember meeting with a teacher who felt that based on her age and social pressures, it was time for her to retire. Yet, it was clear to me that she was not really ready to retire. She was financially prepared, but she loved her job and felt she had more to give.

She spoke to some retired former colleagues, and several of them said they regretted their decision to retire and wished they had continued to work. She decided to keep working and, when she eventually did decide to call it quits, she used her talents to volunteer and teach for a non-profit organization.

If you are feeling conflicted about retiring, seek out three recently retired friends (in the past three years) and ask them the following questions:

- What was the transition like emotionally when you stopped working?
- Would you have done anything differently?
- What was the best advice you received when planning for retirement?

One thing I have noticed from those that have recently retired is that they are more than willing to provide their thoughts on their own transition and pass on the knowledge they have gained along the way to their own Fruitful Retirement. In other words, don't be shy about reaching out to someone you know and asking the above questions. They will appreciate speaking to you about it.

Redefining You

Your retirement, especially in the early days, is a big transitional phase. We as a society often base our identities on what we do for a living. We spend hours each day for decades of our lives working, being a teacher, a police officer, a soldier, an accountant, a doctor, a researcher, a photographer, a writer, a lawyer. Now, suddenly, we are supposed to just walk out the door and be someone else? That is like expecting my five-month-old niece to walk before she crawls. That's just not how it works.

While you never completely stop *being* those things in a way, you will eventually stop *doing* them for money on a regular basis. So, a big part of who you are is removed from your day-to-day life. You may feel that your relevance in life has been challenged.

A successful retirement begins with thinking about how you are going to spend your time and what is going to give you the greatest peace and joy during this journey. You will have to create a new identity, the new "you" you will be for the rest of your life, or until you decide to try out something else.

Can Money Buy Happiness?

You might think that money and abundance—essentially other words for happiness—are correlated. *The more money you have, the happier you are.* Right? It's not that simple.

A 2013 study[1] by the University of Michigan and Brookings Institute looked at people in 25 countries and concluded that those that make more money are more than likely to be happier than those that make less. However, a 2010 study[2] by Princeton economists Daniel Kahneman and Angus Deaton suggests that higher income will improve life evaluation *but not one's emotional well-being.* In other words, a higher income or degree of education will reinforce how you view yourself but not result in better health and social relationships.

While making money is part of the financial independence equation, our behavior around money is more important than the amount. A recently published analysis[3] in the journal

Nature Human Behavior surveyed more than 1.7 million people from 164 countries to put a price on optimal emotional well-being and concluded that people are happiest when they make about $75,000 a year.

You might be surprised that the number isn't higher. I was too. You might also be relieved because $75,000 is a fairly realistic yearly income for many of us. So, it's not just the doctors, lawyers, and hedge fund managers among us that have a shot at happiness.

This study is backed up by what has been researched by economists and psychologists alike for the past quarter-century and is known as the science of money. It is all quite straightforward when you think about it. You see this in action when you read stories about people who win the lottery. They are deliriously happy at first but often lack the understanding and discipline to leverage a better financial future from their windfall. Thus, they spend it quickly and end up where they began and no happier for it.

So that initial rush they get from buying whatever they want *feels* like happiness and, for a while, it brings a sort of euphoria. But they buy and buy and buy until, eventually, the buzz they derived from purchasing material items decreases and the emotional high it used to give them disappears.

This is an extremely important concept to understand because it literally means that our happiness does not come from how much money we make, or what kind of house or car we own.

If it did, then the world's most economically prosperous country, the United States, would be ranked number one as the world's happiest country. However, the 2019 World's Happiness Report[4] listed the U.S. as number 19, with Finland in the top spot. This report was prepared by an international panel of social scientists convened by the UN and edited by top world economists. What did these eminent experts find were the reasons that Finland is statistically the happiest place on earth (sorry Disney World)? Social foundations and trust.

Health is Wealth

While money is an integral part of your retirement plan, it is not a guarantee of good health or abundant life. In fact, good health is the most critical aspect of retirement to most retirees according to a recent survey by Merrill Lynch (81%).[5] I suspect that if you polled the general public, it would rank pretty high for all of us, but because most retirees are in their 60s and older, health matters start to become more important. Even perfectly healthy people can start to feel the impact of aging as they approach the traditional retirement age. That goes for mental as well as physical health.

Ironically, perhaps, even if you are more than ready to leave your career because of the stress or dislike for your company, being employed offers a lot of health benefits. Let's take a look at some of the pros and cons of working when it comes to retirement.

Chapter 4

Weighing Your Options:
Work or Retire?

My life so far has been a long series
of things I wasn't ready for.

– Ashleigh Brilliant

Pros of Working

Working gives us a sense of purpose

We have all heard stories of the idle rich and we might envy certain aspects of their lives: endless vacations to exotic places, shopping sprees, glamorous parties, and so on. But we have also seen the dark side of unlimited wealth: addictions, mental health issues and, in some extreme cases, suicide.

Sure, it might seem enviable to not have to go to work every day, but when you don't have a job, a place to go and make a contribution, how do you fill your time? Some of the independently wealthy fill their time with things like charitable pursuits, but we don't read about them in the tabloids.

Having a sense of purpose in our lives has physical and mental benefits:

Having a sense of purpose in life is associated with a lower risk of death, according to a study published on May 24, 2019, in *JAMA Network Open*.

The research, which sampled almost 7,000 people, included a Psychological Well-Being evaluation—a seven-item questionnaire that assessed purpose in life (Alimujiang, et al, 2019). The researchers concluded: "This study's results indicated that stronger purpose in life was associated with decreased mortality. Purposeful living may have health benefits" (2019, p. 2).[6]

Working gives us a routine

Idle hands are the devil's workshop, so the cliché goes, but being bored can lead to bad habits and depression. You might have experienced a small amount of this if you have ever been unemployed for a length of time or had a couple of weeks off between leaving one job and starting another.

Worry about the loss of income aside, at first, not having to go to work every day is great. You get to sleep in as long as you want, and you have plenty of time to go to the gym, cook nice meals from scratch, run errands when everyone else is at work. It's great … for a while.

And then you get bored. Most or all of your friends and family are at their jobs, so there isn't anyone to do things with during the day. Your house cannot get any cleaner, and you've checked off everything on your to-do list. You realize that you have gone two days without interacting with a single human— or even spoken out loud!

Humans are creatures of habit, and our work routine—get up, shower, go to work, come home, eat dinner, go to bed (or whatever your particular weekday routine happens to be)—is all part of our habits.

Our mental health is better when we have a routine: "Developing a daily routine can help us to feel more in control of everything and help us to make room for all that's important. Routine can aid our mental health. It can help us to cope with change, to form healthy habits, and to reduce our stress levels."[7]

Work allows us to socialize

Even if you do not love all your co-workers, going to work and seeing the same people every day gives us a chance to socialize. It may also expose us to kinds of people we don't have in our personal lives: older people, younger people, people from other countries or areas of the U.S., people from different ethnicities and religions.

According to a 2016 article on Psychologytoday.com, "socializing can provide a number of benefits to your physical and mental health. Did you know that connecting with friends may also boost your brain health and lower your risk of dementia?[8]

Also, the more varied the social groups you have, personal friends, work colleagues, family, hobby groups, and such, the less likely you are to catch colds.[9] So, even if your co-workers are giving you anxiety, they are also keeping you healthy! (It should be noted this was a pre-COVID-19 article and social distancing may apply).

Work gives us a sense of identity

I suppose we could debate whether deriving a sense of identity from your job is a good thing, but there is no denying that for many people what they do for a living is a big part of who and what they are. It is not surprising, then, that what we spend hours a day over decades of our life will become part of our identity.[10]

According to Derek Thompson, "The Gospel of Work," or what he calls *workism*, "is the belief that work is not only necessary to economic production but also the centerpiece of one's identity and life's purpose; and the belief that any policy to promote human welfare must always encourage more work."[11]

As we discussed earlier, losing that sense of identity upon retirement is a difficult adjustment for many people.

Work gives us a break from home

Of course, we love our families and our homes but sometimes we need a break from both. Even the most loving of families will get on each other's nerves sometimes, and when we're at home, it can seem like there is always some chore or project that needs our attention. Spending time at work can help us appreciate our family and home more.

I cannot tell you how many times that I have worked with couples when the non-working spouse eventually tells the recently retired spouse to find another job or something to do because they are around the house too much! Frankly, I think my wife would do the same thing (although she would not admit it!).

At first, I would find it funny, but it makes sense. We are habits of our routines, and while one spouse was working, the other might have been home and free to roam and do their thing without worry about the other spouse at work. However, once both are home at the same time, it results in a different dynamic, and if the recently retired spouse does not have a plan as to how they will be spending their time during the day, this can become an issue. I have one client that retired and leaves the house from 9am – 2pm every weekday as a matter of course to keep some sort of schedule. He does a variety of tasks, from volunteering to mowing lawns to having coffee with friends. He just knew he needed the routine of being out of the house, and I noticed his wife has yet to complain about his schedule.

Cons of Working

You don't choose your schedule

While having a routine is important and beneficial in many ways, having a job means you're beholden to a routine that you didn't choose for yourself. While more and more employers are offering their employees greater flexibility, allowing them to work from home or not enforcing strict start and end times, plenty do not. If you work traditional days, 9 to 5 Monday through Friday, for instance, it can mean you are stuck commuting during rush hour. You perform scheduling gymnastics, arranging things like medical appointments, or dropping off and picking up children from school.

Vacations are also an issue. You can't always take time off when you want to, when your kids are on school break or during the off-season when flights are.

Your time is not your own

Thanks to things like the internet, email, remote work programs, and cell phones, we can often feel like we are never really off of work even when we're not physically there. No matter how much you enjoy your job, you do not want to be connected to it 24/7. Constantly being available for work can create tension among family and friends too. Nothing ruins a date night or happy hour like having to excuse yourself to take a call from your boss.

You are tied to a location

As I mentioned above, although more employers are allowing their employees to work remotely, it is still a relatively new concept and there will always be jobs that cannot be done off site. That means you are stuck in your current location. Now, that is not always a bad thing. Maybe you love where you live.

But if you do not, it has real impact on your quality of life. A great way to move up your retirement timeline is to move to an area with a lower cost of living.

As I am writing this, we are dealing with the COVID-19 health crisis, and this will completely redefine the next decade in many areas, one of which is flexible and remote working practices. I see employers redefining their workplaces, based on their industry and technological capability, in ways that may allow for greater flexibility to the pending retiree who is willing to continue working without geographic limitations.

This restriction may soon become a thing of the past, and over time we will move into a new normal. Yet, if you really do like what you do, but just don't want to do it for 40 hours per week in the same place, it does not hurt to ask your employer what options are available. Just ask yourself, if you were in your employer's shoes, would you want to keep you as an employee?

Of course!

(Hint: if you answered No to that question, you should be looking for another job.)

You work with people you don't like

And even if you do like your boss and most of your co-workers, think about how much time you spend with them every day, week, month, and year. You spend more time with the people you work with than you do with members of your own family, and probably far more than you get to spend with your friends.

Now, there will be conflict. And, of course, it is multiplied when you don't like the people you work with. This one reminds me of the comedy show *The Office* back in the day.

It was hilarious, and its primary focus was on the often-funny relationships that develop while working with people day in and day out.

Pros of Retirement

You choose your schedule

When you retire, you are not on anyone else's timetable (well, maybe your spouse's!). You don't want to get out of bed until 11:00 am? No one can make you. You want to spend 90 minutes in the gym (Hey, some of us do!)? Take all the time you want. You want to go on vacation from September 17th through November 1st? Great, book the flight or take your time driving to get there. I am told the East Coast beaches are best visited in September. You see the point. This is the essence of retirement—being able to do what you want when you want.

Your time is your own

You will still have obligations after you have retired, but you will not constantly be checking emails or logging into the system to troubleshoot a problem. You can fully enjoy what you are doing without work intruding. Being able to put all your energy into the moment not only allows you to more thoroughly enjoy what you are doing, but there are actually many health benefits to doing so. If you ever wanted to quit something, such as smoking, you have a higher likelihood of achieving that goal without the added stress of a job or work deadlines. If you have a goal to lose weight or eat a certain way, having control over your own time is a remarkable help.

This is a great chance to take on big projects, or bold initiatives. When your time is your own, working out gets easier, food tastes better (and you eat less of it, I'm told), you do things more efficiently, and life takes on new meaning. You can become better at whatever it is you desire to be better at because you have control over your time now.

You're mobile!

You can move wherever you want after you retire. Many people choose to downsize their homes once all the kids are grown and out of the house, but you can make a bigger change. More than a few Americans decide to become expats in their retirement, moving to countries with a slower pace of life, a (much) lower cost of living, or better climate. If you are considering this route, you have one more reason to benefit from a team of experts. The thought of moving to another country, for example, will precipitate many questions, ranging from the legal to tax ramifications to your portfolio, so having guidance in these areas will not only save your time, it will provide information to make the best decisions for your life.

At the end of the book I provide a list of Forbes Top 25 Places to Retire from 2019, and added one more that I found to be wonderful.

No more jerks!

Just kidding! Well, sort of. Think of that one person you will be glad to never see again after your last day of work. I remember my first internship when I was in college. The first week I was to shadow a long-term employee who had been with the company for 40 years. He was retiring the following year, and I got the impression he was not well liked across the department. While I was young and eager to learn, I noticed he was not nearly so eager to teach at this juncture of his career, especially when the clock struck 5pm.

One day as he was opening the mail, he kept saying to himself "File 13 ... File 13" and putting much of what he was receiving into a separate pile. Eager to learn, but not wanting to show my inadequacy in remembering all the acronyms at the company (a story for another book), I hesitantly asked what I should do with the "File 13" documents. He pointed to the trash with his middle finger and a look of disdain.

Yes, I am sure you can think of a story or two that would bring a smile to your face when you move on.

You can pursue hobbies

Most of us have a hobby that we enjoy—cooking, photography, painting, antiquing—that we never have as much time as we want to spend on. Now you can pursue that hobby to your heart's content. Your hobbies can be a great way to make new social connections, give you a sense of purpose, and evolve a new sense of self, all things you lose when you stop working. If you currently have no hobby, start thinking of some things you would be interested in trying out. Remember, you have a lot of time to fill and hobbies are a great way to fill it.

At the end of the book I have listed 100 things to do in retirement. Take a look and maybe some ideas will come of it.

Cons of Retirement

You can lose your sense of purpose

I have described how work provides a sense of purpose and how retirement can leave us without one. That is why it is so important to find something like a hobby to provide a purpose. A recent study published in *The Journal of the American Medical Association*[12] indicates that a stronger purpose in life is associated with lower mortality. Purpose comes in many forms, whether it is at your church, as a community volunteer, a grandparent, using your knowledge to teach others a skill, or just doing something that adds to the quality of your life and is personally satisfying. It is not so much the activity that matters as the sense of purpose that it brings.

I live in a small town named Carlisle, PA. We have a healthy number of very active retirees in our community, volunteering and serving on board positions ranging from the Rotary Club of Carlisle to the United Way. At our local Saint Patrick's Church, I know many that are involved in any number of our 25 different ministries. I like to call my mom the baby whisperer because of her uncanny ability to make every baby in her presence smile. As such, she volunteers to work with the children of our congregation from birth to school age.

You lose your daily routine

When your days are open-ended, you can feel like you are just drifting along. This can be great at first; you have nowhere to be and can do whatever you want. In the first few days or weeks, or even months, of retirement, you love it. It is so freeing! But without a routine, you can quickly become bored and fall into bad habits.

Years ago, I remember Colin Powell giving a TED Talk[13] about the importance of parents infusing structure into their children's lives. This rubbed against the grain of thought that held that it stunted their creativity. The fact is, however, that it provides a sense of structure and familiarity. Adults are no different, and having a daily routine will empower them to take ownership of the activity and offer structure to the days ahead.

We are no doubt creatures of habit. It is why I do not need an alarm to wake me up in the morning, or why I have my coffee when I do not need the caffeine. Benjamin Franklin once stated, "Your net worth to the world is usually determined by what remains after your bad habits are subtracted from your good ones." I like that statement.

Once you know your purpose, and set up a routine around it, there is an automated efficiency to your life that will benefit you.

You lose an important part of your social network

If you were close to your colleagues outside of work before you retired, you may still see them, only not nearly as much. This can leave a big gap in your social life. When you do see them, you might feel out of the loop when they fill you in on office politics that have lost their relevance for you.

One of my dear friends and clients retired not too long ago. She is one that just cannot sit still. You all know that kind of person, and you may even be that person. I am married to one (and so is she, so I cannot say much). Well, she moved across the country, so she had to recreate her social network. Since she is a go-getter and just loves to live life, she signed up on Meetup.com. It is an online community that allows anyone to create a platform based on what they love to do and where they live and connect with others in their local community that share the same interests. It is a wonderful way to get connected and have fun.

Speaking of staying connected, I know that if I visit a number of local breakfast or coffee establishments on certain mornings (Panera Bread, McDonald's, and the local diners know this), I will see groups of retired men hanging out and socializing, enjoying each other's company. (I imagine that by lunchtime they have solved the world's social and political problems).

You can lose your identity

I discussed this earlier. Losing your career, even when it is by choice, means losing a big part of who you have been for decades. This is how you are viewed by others, how you may view yourself, and what has provided relevance to your life. It is not confined to a specific career or industry. This can affect all of us and cannot be overstated.

Having worked with many clients over the years that have served in the military, I noticed that when each of them retired from their branch of service, it was very similar to a civilian person retiring from their employment. The difference is most of them went back into the workforce due to their age and continued interest in utilizing their skills. The interesting part of this is when they finally retired for good; the transition into their next chapter was smoother because they had essentially already done it once before.

Not all of us will have a dry run at this, but the activity is the same. We all plan to do it sooner or later, so put some time into becoming aware of who you are and what your identity is now prior to retirement, and what you want it to become. The great news is that retirement is not the end, but the beginning of a new life!

You're always at home!

This can cause a lot of friction between you and your spouse. Absence makes the heart grow fonder, and familiarity breeds contempt. This is not something to overlook. I have seen it often, where, after a month of being retired, one spouse is browsing the internet for a job to get the other out of the house for part of the day. This becomes an issue when the partner who is not working has their own routine that is now being affected by the retiree looking for things to do all day.

This is another reason why creating a routine is helpful for everybody. It is also important to include activities you plan to do alone, as well as those you plan to do together.

You're not the boss

If you have been in a senior position for many years, used to telling people what to do and seeing them do it, you might be in for a rude awakening if you expect the same at home. The people in your household have their ways of doing things that you haven't been aware of, and they will not take kindly to your interference. An example of this in my life is when I first got married.

The first week after our honeymoon, she was making me breakfast. It was great! As I watched her go back and forth from the refrigerator to the counter for the eggs, then the bread, then waiting to cook the eggs until the bacon was done, and so on, I noticed that she could save time by doing things a different way.

So, being the kind of person that tends to analyze behavior and finds joy in helping others, I suggested a new-and-improved method to my wife and the following week was back to cooking my own breakfast.

I learned quickly. You may have to re-learn as well.

You lose your income

Of course, working comes with its own expenses, but the money you save on things like commuting and dry cleaning are nothing compared to the money you lose when you are no longer receiving a paycheck. You might have millions of dollars saved for retirement and know that the chances of running out before you run out of years are nearly non-existent. But it is that *nearly* that can keep you up at night.

Thus, I am a firm believer in engaging a professional that does retirement income planning for a living. That advisor will have a level of perception from years of experience working with other families going through the same transition that would be difficult for you to acquire. Most importantly, it will give you clarity on the financial side of what you need to do now and in the future.

Chapter 5

What to Do with Your Time

*Everyone should have the experience of getting lost
in life at least once. Part of growing up is learning
how to tolerate uncertainty, and when the time is
right, to find or create a new path for yourself.*

– Cole Todd

Finding New Opportunities

The good news—the *really* good news—is that you can negate all the cons of no longer working while reaping the benefits of having a job during your retirement. There is a wealth of proof that staying active in retirement will result in a healthier and happier experience.

The reason many financially independent people decide to continue their employment in some capacity is the ability to socialize, which allows one to stay relevant in an ever-changing world and stay connected. The key here is to first identify what it is that you truly enjoy doing. What makes you feel good?

Maslow's hierarchy of needs identifies the basic necessities of life: food, shelter, water, security, and safety. Once these needs are adequately met, we can begin to focus on belonging and self-esteem, eventually working toward our true potential as humans, which gives us a focus outside of ourselves. As the saying goes, "What a man can be, he must be."

What do you want to do now that you have the time? If you struggle to answer that, ask yourself what you wanted to do when you were 20 or 30 or 40? A lot of people have what their parents or friends or society deem "unrealistic" dreams about what they would like to do with their lives when they're young. Take being an artist for example: not many parents are going to be thrilled to hear their kid wants to go to art school (apologies to my cousin who is an extremely talented artist).

Maybe you wanted to be a teacher but decided there was not enough money in it to support the kind of life you wanted. There is nothing wrong with wanting to make a lot of money and choosing a career that pays well, but that big-money career may never be as satisfying to you as teaching.

Your skills learned over the years may provide you an opportunity to teach others via speaking engagements, consulting, or even writing a book. Passing on knowledge is good for the soul (and one reason why I am writing this book). You could go back to school and take an online class on a subject that always interested you. Or you could become an online tutor. There are online tutoring companies for many subjects and for students of all ages. Many of these opportunities don't require a teaching certificate, but most do require a college degree in the field. Online tutoring would also allow you to work from home and give you more (but usually not total) control of your schedule.

Perhaps you would have liked to leave your career and start your own business when you were in your 30s or 40s, but you had all of those "grown-up" things by then: a spouse, a mortgage, a kid or two. You felt that it would be irresponsible to leave the security of a job to strike out on your own.

The second question to ask yourself is if money were not a concern, what would you do? It's 10am on a Wednesday. What are you doing? It's 3pm on Monday. Where are you?

You have the freedom now to do whatever you want. You can start painting or drawing or sculpting, whatever your artistic medium is. Do you want to make a little money at it? You can create an Etsy or Shopify store, set up a booth at a craft fair, or create an Amazon page.

You may not want to start a business in the traditional sense during retirement. Starting a business is a lot of work and you are probably looking to work less. But could you start an online business? Maybe you want to open an antique store. What do you need to do that? A brick-and-mortar space and a lot of inventory to fill it? That's a pretty expensive proposition. Instead, you can sell antiques online at sites like eBay, Ruby Lane, or ArtFire.

Money isn't everything, of course, and some of you are in a position where it doesn't matter if you bring in money during retirement. A great way to achieve that is to volunteer.

Volunteering keeps you in regular contact with others and helps you develop a solid support system, which in turn protects you against depression. Volunteering makes you happy. By measuring hormones and brain activity, researchers have discovered that being helpful to others delivers immense pleasure.[14]

Maybe you don't want to do any kind of work at all after you retire. And there's nothing wrong with that. But to live a fruitful life, you will need to find some way to occupy your time and fill all the voids left when you no longer have a job.

You Are Not Alone in This

If you have a spouse or partner, you need to consider them in all of this before you start making grand plans for the future. You might be ready to sell the house and pull up stakes for a beach in Central America while your spouse has other ideas.

This time can be a tough transition for both of you. If your spouse does not work, it can feel like you're constantly underfoot. If your spouse is still working, your new schedule can be problematic. Maybe you like to stay up late now that you don't have to be up at any particular time and you're making all sorts of racket that makes it hard for them to sleep. Or, maybe you have been home, bored all day, and as soon as your spouse walks through the door, you pounce. You may be grateful to finally have someone to talk to, but they may be accustomed to getting home before you and having a little quiet time to unwind before engaging.

If money has never been an issue and your spouse is used to spending whatever they want, the sudden need to reign that spending in, now that there is no longer a paycheck coming in, can cause a lot of tension. This is especially true when you have been the one to handle the money in your relationship without much input from your spouse. That should never have happened in the first place, and it is going to have to change as you move into retirement.

People cannot be expected to understand what has never been explained to them, so sit down with your spouse and discuss where you are financially. If you need help or feel the two of you cannot have this discussion without it blowing up, call your financial advisor. This is a perfect job for them.

Retirement is a new stage for both of you, and you have to treat it that way. Do the exercises at the end of this chapter on your own and then together if you have a partner.

The purpose of this book is to focus on creating and living the Fruitful life, and the ability to adopt solid financial habits early in life goes a long way toward the creation of wealth and freedom. This allows the ability to spend your time and energy living out your reason for being in this world. Designing your Fruitful Retirement is a blend of art and math, fused together to create a purpose in your life that is financially sustainable.

If you are looking to retire in the next few years, there is no time like the present to take a deep dive into your behavior toward money because once you do turn off the lever of employment, the wealth you have created is what you must work with to live the rest of your life, so align your behavior of money with what truly brings you happiness.

If you know how you want to spend your time, you can better plan to spend your money.

Let's begin by answering the five questions on the next page. It is very important to take your time with each of these exercises to look inward. It will greatly help you in the last exercise of the chapter and enhances your clarity when determining your fruit. Do not move forward with the book until you have completed these exercises.

After answering those five questions, move on to filling out the four quadrants regarding both your work and personal lives. Fill out the squares with an honest assessment of your likes, dislikes, and abilities.

Answer the following questions:

┌─── WHAT DO YOU LOVE ABOUT LIFE? ───┐

└────────────────────────────────────┘

┌─── WHAT IS IMPORTANT ABOUT LIFE TO YOU? ───┐

└────────────────────────────────────┘

┌─── WHAT BRINGS YOU THE MOST JOY AND
HAPPINESS IN YOUR EVERYDAY ACTIVITIES? ───┐

└────────────────────────────────────┘

┌─ IF YOU HAD MORE TIME DURING THE DAY, WHICH
ACTIVITIES WOULD YOU SPEND MORE TIME DOING? ─┐

└────────────────────────────────────┘

┌─── MAKE A LIST OF GOALS AND PRIORITIZE THEM ───┐

└────────────────────────────────────┘

Fill out the squares as an honest assessment of your life:

	DISLIKE	LIKE
GOOD OR SKILLED		
NOT GOOD OR UNSKILLED		

If you happen to find that your work life is in the bottom left quadrant, then you should be searching for a new career. Life is too short. Enjoy what you do and be good at it. If you really love doing it, but are not good at it, make it a hobby or get good at it as fast as you can.

Ideally, your personal life should be focused on the top right. Notwithstanding, there be may something in the bottom right quadrant that you have always wanted to increase your knowledge, sharpen your skill, or frankly understand. It is best to accept that you will never be great at this activity but take joy in doing it. Golf comes to mind for me.

While an excess of time would allow me to play more with an expectation of getting lower scores, I am keenly aware of my limitations in this sport. Yet, I accept it and play for enjoyment and not necessarily to improve my skill. It is why it is a hobby and not a career.

The art of creating The Fruitful Retirement starts with knowing yourself and how you desire to spend your time. Just as sand is part of the beach, so is your money with retirement, but more sand alone does not enhance the experience. It is who you are with, what you are doing, and how you are enjoying it. I am reminded of the lyrics from Zac Brown's song "Chicken Fried":

It's funny how it's the little things in life that mean the most. Not where you live, what you drive, or the price tag on your clothes. There's no dollar sign on a peace of mind, this I've come to know.[15]

Such is life once you have stopped your traditional work life. The goal of this chapter is to help you determine what you are going to do with your time. These activities should bring you clarity and joy, not stress you out.

The normal way to talk about retirement is to think about how much of your income needs to be replaced. While we will discuss that later in the book, what gets lost in translation but is no less important is how you replace your time.

The next two pages show two open calendars. The first is for your current schedule, and the second is for your future schedule. You may want to make a copy as you may need to do a few drafts of your future schedule. Take a few minutes to complete the activity below.

1. Write down your daily schedule from when you wake up in the morning until bedtime during the days you are employed. Review it for completeness.

2. Now take any activities that you still plan on doing in retirement and write them in Calendar 2, your future schedule.

3. Once complete, you will see the openings you need to fill in your future calendar. It is up to you to flesh out your days to come with activities that bring you joy.

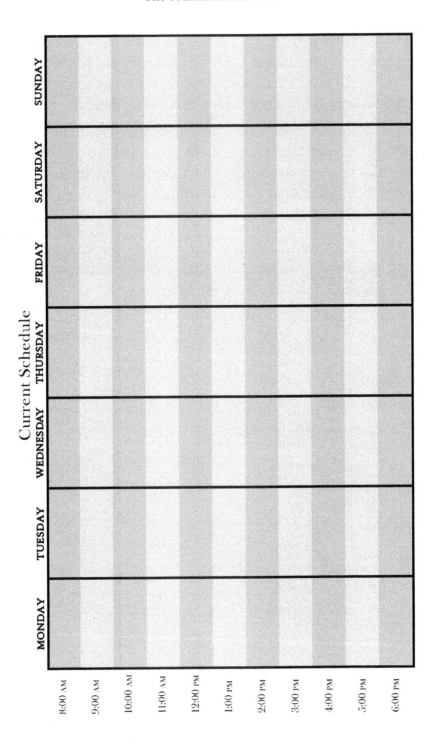

Current Schedule

	MONDAY	TUESDAY	WEDNESDAY	THURSDAY	FRIDAY	SATURDAY	SUNDAY
8:00 AM							
9:00 AM							
10:00 AM							
11:00 AM							
12:00 PM							
1:00 PM							
2:00 PM							
3:00 PM							
4:00 PM							
5:00 PM							
6:00 PM							

Future Schedule

	MONDAY	TUESDAY	WEDNESDAY	THURSDAY	FRIDAY	SATURDAY	SUNDAY
8:00 AM							
9:00 AM							
10:00 AM							
11:00 AM							
12:00 PM							
1:00 PM							
2:00 PM							
3:00 PM							
4:00 PM							
5:00 PM							
6:00 PM							

Hopefully you have spent some time truly contemplating what you love about life and what is important to you. This should have helped you think about some of the activities that you would like to spend more time doing because of the joy they bring. From there, it was natural to prioritize a list of short-term goals, with the final exercise of completing a calendar giving you a look at your allocation of time after retirement.

Now you are ready to determine your fruit.

Part II

DETERMINING YOUR FRUIT

Most of us are familiar with the old USDA Food Pyramid. It is outdated now, debunked by our better understanding of nutrition, but a pyramid is a good visual to help you determine which fruit you are. From there we will know how to proceed with your plan for a Fruitful Retirement.

The Fruitful Retirement pyramid is made up of three parts: Needs, Wants, and Legacy.

Needs

This is the base of our pyramid, our foundation, our soil. If we do not have enough income to create a stable base, our pyramid will not stand, or, our soil will be unhealthy, and our plants will not produce fruit. Needs are the things we must pay for: housing, food, utilities, and health care.

Wants

If we have healthy soil, our Needs are met, and we reap a harvest sufficient to fulfill most of our Wants. Very few of us have enough money to realistically satisfy *all* our Wants, but this is meant to be a realistic goal of things that we would enjoy having and doing.

Legacy

Once our Needs and Wants are met, our plans can reach for the sky and create a Legacy for our family or the causes we care about. I often say that 'to give is to receive'. I truly would love every one of you to be in the financial position that all your Needs and Wants might be covered so that you can focus your time and energy on giving back. Note that I just said "your time and energy" not your money. While it is absolutely wonderful to give back financially, whether it be in tithes or another form of charitable contribution, my point is that having a solid financial foundation frees you to devote your creativity, intellect, strength, and will to things that bring you and others joy.

These three things make up each fruit type but in different proportions according to the shape of the fruit. To determine which fruit you are, you will need to do the budget exercise found later in the book.

If you are not retired yet, you will not have exact numbers to work with, but the budget you use now will give you fairly accurate numbers. Do not make the mistake of underestimating your retirement spending. Most retirees find that their expenses decrease during retirement because they are no longer paying for things like commuting expenses, a work wardrobe and, of course, there are no longer 401k, Medicare, and Social Security withholdings.

But others will see an increase in spending once they retire. They finally have the time to do the traveling they have long wanted to do, they may encounter more medical expenses, and they may find that shopping is a great way to fill their free time.

A common rule of thumb suggests that you will need 70 to 80% of your pre-retirement income to pay the bills. I would steer clear of this rule of thumb. The term 'rule of thumb' was coined by brewers as a method by which to test the temperature of a batch of beer. Instead of the brewer's thumb to estimate your expenses, wouldn't you rather use your own?

We *will* incorporate other sound, well-established, and generally accepted rules of thumb later. But for now, I want you to understand that there is no one-size-fits-all retirement plan.

Creating a retirement plan based on someone else's suggested figures just does not make sense. For us to determine which fruit we are, we first must complete a budget.

Planning and Budgeting

"To steer is heaven, to drift, hell" sums up why planning for retirement, and anything else really, is so important. Proper planning puts you in control, and when you are in control you have less fear.

Your budget will be your roadmap. A retirement budget is no different than a budget in any other stage in your life. It shows you how much money is coming in, how much is going out, and where it's going. The only difference now is that the money coming in is not coming from your paycheck but from your sources of guaranteed income and investments.

It is common for your budget to change over time. My experience with clients suggests that they spend more in their 60s than their 70s, and even less in their 80s and beyond—with the exception of a healthcare situation requiring significant out-of-pocket costs. We will talk about this later, but for now, it is important to know that it is reasonable to plan for a higher spending in your Wants category early in retirement.

Having and sticking to an appropriate budget is a cornerstone of personal finance at every stage of life, but it is never more important than it is during retirement. The younger we are, the easier it is to pivot and to live with some degree of discomfort.

Not bringing in enough money when you are 25? Change jobs. We all know that you almost always get a bigger income boost by changing jobs than you do by getting a raise at your current job. Or use your evenings and weekends to bring in extra money with a side hustle. Move into a smaller place. You have not yet acquired all the family members and accoutrements that fill up the house (to say nothing of the attic, basement, garage, shed, and storage units) of people a few years older. Or stay in your current place but rent out one of the spare bedrooms. Boom.

If we chose not to continue working in some capacity during retirement, we normally aren't getting a raise. We are a lot less willing to make do or feel lifestyle discomfort the older we get. You don't want to move into a smaller place, and the idea of having a roommate may not be ideal (although I do believe the

Golden Girls were decades ahead of their time with the idea of shared living). Getting your budget right during retirement is a must. People always talk about the risk to your investments during retirement, but that is not the real risk.

Risk is not having money when you need it. Risk is not a part of your portfolio dropping 20% in a given quarter; it is not knowing how much you spend or not having a plan to generate sufficient income for future expenses.

To plan for the risk of running out of money, you must start with a plan. That plan must start with the monies you Need. It then moves onto the monies you Want, and finally to the monies you would like to give away. The best way to start this process is to complete a budget.

There are two ways to budget: top-down and bottom-up. Top-down is a great way to budget when you are in the accumulation phase of your life because it works on the premise of paying yourself first. You put a certain amount of money into your emergency fund, your insurance policy, and your investments (20% of your gross salary is a good solid goal during the accumulation phase of your life), and you can spend whatever is left after that.

However, there are certain times in your life when you really should do a bottom-up budget—that is, you look at all the expenses going out each month, quarter, or year, and you write those down. Hold that amount aside—save and invest the rest.

The cool thing is, there are so many tools out there that allow you to aggregate your expenses in any given year. Most advisors have data aggregation tools. FinTech online options allow you to do this as well. In fact, if you use certain credit cards, they will segregate your expenses at the end of the year for you. If you prefer to go old school and do it by hand, that works just fine and still my preference when budgeting.

It should not be hard to look at a year-end statement and see where your money goes. That is the first step: to see where your money goes. When we think of budgeting, we think of it as a means to an end. That end is ensuring that we have what we need to sustain a comfortable lifestyle. Then, from that we can ask how we create a sustainable income stream that will last as long as we're here on Earth.

Building your budget is your next assignment. I have created a template to help you get it right. You actually have to do a few versions. The first is for you, or you and your partner. The second is for the remaining spouse after the primary bread winner dics (if applicable). Does the death of the bread winner change which type of fruit the remaining spouse will be? Will they go from an Apple to a Pear with no assets to provide a sustainable income stream? No one wants that for their surviving spouse.

Please complete the retirement budget below, as it will be used in the next section when we determine our fruit. If you are married or have a partner, then choose who is 'C1' and who is 'C2'. You will notice income is separated but expenses are combined. If single, separated, or widowed, you would be 'C1'.

You will use the same method for the survivor retirement budget if it applies to your situation, just with different inputs. Each spouse or partner should complete their own, using figures assuming their partner has passed on.

The beauty of The Fruitful Retirement is its simplicity in visualizing both your retirement and survivor plan in a similar manner.

Joint
Retirement Budget

MONTHLY INCOME	C1	C2
Social Security		
Annuity		
Real Estate		
Military Retirement		
Federal Pension		
Company Pension		
Other Pension		
SubTotal		
Total Monthly Income		

MONTHLY EXPENSES		
Needs		
Cable/Internet		
Car Fuel		
Car Insurance		
Car Maintenance		
Groceries		
Health Insurance		
Homeowner's Insurance		
House Payment (P&I)		
House/Property Taxes		
Phone		
Life Insurance		
Long Term Care Insurance		
Medical Expenses		
Renter's Insurance		
Utilities		
Other Needs		
Total Needs		

Wants		
Car Payment		
Church/Charity		
Dining Out		
Hobbies		
Organizational Dues		
Travel		
Other Entertainment		
Total Wants		

Legacy		
Gifts to Family		
Other		
Total Legacy		

MONTHLY BUDGET	C1 & C2
Total Monthly Income*	
Total Monthly Needs	
Needs Surplus/Shortfall	
Total Monthly Wants	
Wants Surplus/Shortfall	
Total Monthly Legacy	
Legacy Surplus/Shortfall	

*After tax monthly income

MONTHLY INCOME	
	Surviving Spouse
Social Security	
Annuity	
Real Estate	
Military Retirement	
Federal Pension	
Company Pension	
Other Pension	
Total Monthly Income	

Surviving Spouse Retirement Budget 1

MONTHLY EXPENSES	
Needs	
Cable/Internet	
Car Fuel	
Car Insurance	
Car Maintenance	
Groceries	
Health Insurance	
Homeowner's Insurance	
House Payment (P&I)	
House/Property Taxes	
Phone	
Life Insurance	
Long Term Care Insurance	
Medical Expenses	
Renter's Insurance	
Utilities	
Other Needs	
Total Needs	
Wants	
Car Payment	
Church/Charity	
Dining Out	
Hobbies	
Organizational Dues	
Travel	
Other Entertainment	
Total Wants	
Legacy	
Gifts to Family	
Other	
Total Legacy	

MONTHLY BUDGET	
	Surviving Spouse
Total Monthly Income*	
Total Monthly Needs	
Needs Surplus/Shortfall	
Total Monthly Wants	
Wants Surplus/Shortfall	
Total Monthly Legacy	
Legacy Surplus/Shortfall	

*After tax monthly income

MONTHLY INCOME

	Surviving Spouse
Social Security	
Annuity	
Real Estate	
Military Retirement	
Federal Pension	
Company Pension	
Other Pension	
Total Monthly Income	

MONTHLY EXPENSES

Needs

Cable/Internet	
Car Fuel	
Car Insurance	
Car Maintenance	
Groceries	
Health Insurance	
Homeowner's Insurance	
House Payment (P&I)	
House/Property Taxes	
Phone	
Life Insurance	
Long Term Care Insurance	
Medical Expenses	
Renter's Insurance	
Utilities	
Other Needs	
Total Needs	

Wants

Car Payment	
Church/Charity	
Dining Out	
Hobbies	
Organizational Dues	
Travel	
Other Entertainment	
Total Wants	

Legacy

Gifts to Family	
Other	
Total Legacy	

Surviving Spouse Retirement Budget 2

MONTHLY BUDGET

	Surviving Spouse
Total Monthly Income*	
Total Monthly Needs	
Needs Surplus/Shortfall	
Total Monthly Wants	
Wants Surplus/Shortfall	
Total Monthly Legacy	
Legacy Surplus/Shortfall	

*After tax monthly income

Which Fruit Are You?

Let's look again at the pyramid.

Our budgeting priorities are allocated in different proportions to each of the three categories: Needs, Wants, and Legacy. Now, we are going to superimpose three fruits—Pears, Apples, and Strawberries—onto our pyramid. Your fruit is determined by the location of your budgeting priorities on the pyramid.

We relate our three fruits to the pyramid above such that a pear is thickest at the bottom, an apple is thickest in the middle, and a strawberry is thickest at the top. Consequently, Pears are the bottom of the pyramid, Apples in the middle, and Strawberries at the top.

<u>**Your fruit is determined by the area of the pyramid where your income stream falls short.**</u>

If your income sources, such as Social Security and pensions, do not cover your Needs, you are a Pear, since you are at a shortfall at the lowest level of the pyramid, where it is broadest.

Which Fruit are You?

Similarly, if the income you receive in retirement covers all your Needs but not all your Wants, then you are an Apple, as your focus should be in the middle section of the pyramid.

You are a Strawberry if all your income covers your Needs and Wants, and therefore your focus should be at the top of the pyramid, where the strawberry is broadest.

Get it?

You can only fall into one category at a time. That said, Pears can become Apples, and Apples can become Strawberries, depending on the level of income sources at a particular time.

Chapter 6

Pears

A pear is a failed apple.

– George Carlin

What if SS & Pensions are not Enough?

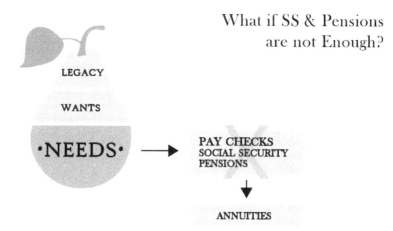

Pears are bigger at the base and get smaller towards the top. They need to prioritize meeting their retirement income needs with guaranteed income sources like pensions and private annuities.

Questions Pears need to answer:

1. What to do if my Social Security and pensions are not enough to cover my Needs?
2. When do I need the income?
3. How much will it take to meet my Needs?
4. How can I mitigate retirement risks?

You will be able to see from the budget exercise you just completed whether you have enough guaranteed income to cover your Needs. "Cover your Needs with guarantees" is the way I put it to my clients. This guaranteed income will meet your basic expenses every month the way your paycheck does during your working life. It is a certain amount of money that you can depend on each month.

What if your budget shows that you do not have enough guaranteed income to meet your Needs? There is no need to panic. You may have enough assets that we can look to for a solution. When I work with clients in this situation, we look at their portfolio and often use some of those assets to buy a pension or annuity in an attempt to have enough guaranteed income.

What happens if we can't do that? You will have to make some tough decisions. You may have to downsize your home, move to an area with a lower cost of living, make some considerable slashes to current expenses, and revisit your activities and the costs associated with them. It may also mean that you can't retire at the age you had hoped to—at least not entirely.

For Pears that have minimal investments, if you need long-term care, you are very likely going to have to rely on Medicaid.

See below for an example of a Pear. In the household below, C1 represents Client 1, and C2 represents Client 2.

There are a few ways to generate the income necessary for Pear. With a Pear we are talking about not having enough guaranteed income to cover their Needs. That is very important and different than an Apple, who will have some flexibility by altering their Wants in times of economic despair or shocks to the financial system.

The Pear must focus on providing guaranteed income sources to match the guaranteed liabilities. We want to provide

Pears Retirement Worksheet

Income Source	C1 & C2 Live
Pension	$3,500
Pension	$0
SS@FRA	$2,750
SS@FRA	$1,500
Total	$7.850
Income Goal	C1 & C2 Live
Needs	$9,000
Shortfall	-$1,150

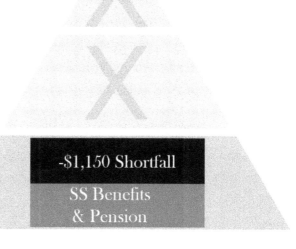

the security and peace of mind in knowing that their Needs are covered. In fact, when I have given presentations to large groups, I sometimes ask if anyone has a pension. Normally, some hands go up, especially from the older attendees in the audience. I then ask if they like having a pension. Not one person dislikes getting a guaranteed income steam for life.

If they don't have a pension—and even if they do—to guarantee the Pear's Needs with an income source, we need to look at something called an annuity. Some of you may have cringed at that word, as I have heard some negative views toward annuities over the years. In fact, I know that the word is like kryptonite to Superman for some of my CPA friends due to misperceptions from the past.

Annuities are just like other financial products, where they can serve a place in the right situation. Some clients should purchase an annuity. Some should not. Some clients may not need to own an annuity as part of their plan but prefer to own stocks for potentially greater long-term return without the mitigated risk.

Regardless of your view up to this point, I would suggest that a Pear view an annuity like paying off their mortgage. There is something wonderful about owning your home free and clear. It is an accomplishment that I was proud of, yes, but more importantly, there is security in knowing that it cannot be taken from you (as long as you pay your taxes on it, of course). The same can be said about knowing that when your necessary bills come due, you have the same level of security. This is why Pears should focus on guaranteed income.

The following chart shows the various types of annuities. Each has a different focus, depending on the time until the income is needed and your risk comfort level. The annuities have been divided between those that provide an immediate income and those that are meant to provide an income stream down the road. The immediate income is known as an immediate annuity. Essentially, a lump sum of money from the investor is paid to the insurance carrier, and in return the insurance carrier provides an income stream for however long was setup in the contract. These options vary and there would be different reasons to choose different terms for each contract.

When will I need income?

	Immediate Income Need	Delayed Income Need		
Product Type	Single Premium Immediate Annuity	Fixed or Indexed Annuity	Deferred Income Annuity	Variable Annuity
Income Time Horizon	Immediate Income	Typically 2-10 Years		Typically 10+ Years
Risk Comfort Zone	Conservative	Conservative to Moderate		Moderate to Aggressive
How It Works	Guaranteed Immediate Income	-Downside Protection -Gtd. Growth -Lifetime Gtd. Income		-Growth -Lifetime Gtd. Income

Fixed and Variable annuities may be suitable for those seeking long-term investing, such as retirement investing. Gains from tax-deferred investments are taxable as ordinary income upon withdrawal. Variable annuities are subject to market risk and may lose value.

Fixed Indexed Annuities (FIA) are not suitable for all investors. FIAs permit investors to participate in only a stated percentage of an increase in an index (participation rate) and may impose a maximum annual account value percentage increase. FIAs typically do not allow for participation in dividends accumulated on the securities represented by the index.

Guarantees are based on the claims paying ability of the issuing company. Withdrawals made prior to age 59 ½ are subject to a 10% IRS penalty tax and surrender charges may apply.

Annuities that are meant to provide an income stream for later in life come in different forms, such as a fixed annuity, fixed indexed, deferred income, or variable annuity. Variable annuities can now be structured with a 'floor' or 'buffer' to help with partially limiting an investor's downside while allowing a higher upside than an indexed annuity. There are also life insurance products that can be added to this mix that can offer an income stream for the retiree to supplement their retirement income plan.

For purposes of this book, we will be focusing on the immediate income annuity and the deferred income annuity. This is to simplify and add clarity to the process. I have included a few traits for each, but this book is not meant to take a deep dive into the types and operations of annuities. Rather, I have included this so you are aware that each annuity is different and "like a box of chocolates—you never know what you are going to get." So, it is very important to work with a professional that understands these products.

While all annuity products have their own twist (you will ultimately want to work with a professional to help sort out which particular product and insurance carrier will be the best fit), shown below are a few calculations to give you an idea of how much of your assets may be needed to generate a certain level of income. It should be noted that the income estimates would be gross, or pre-tax, income.

A single premium immediate annuity (SPIA) is a guaranteed income payment that starts right away, while the deferred options are for a future point in time (i.e., the income will start in 5 or 10 years).

Asset Commitment Rules of Thumb

Single Premium Immediate Annuity - Rule of 225*:
Take the monthly income need and multiply by 225.
Example: $1,150 x 225 = $258,750

Deferred Income Annuity -5 Years - Rule of 165*:
Take the monthly income need and multiply by 165.
Example: $1,150 x 165 = $189,750

Deferred Income Annuity -10 Years - Rule of 125*:
Take the monthly income need and multiply by 125.
Example: $1,150 x 125 = $143,750

*Rule of thumb based on joint income for clients age 65. Rule of thumb numbers are not exact and vary based on age, time horizon, and product. Please consult a financial advisor for numbers specific to your situation.

Content in this material is for general information only and not intended to provide specific advice or recommendations for any individual.

All hypothetical examples listed are not representative of any specific investment. Your results may vary.

Investing includes risks, including fluctuating prices and loss of principal. No strategy assures success or protects against loss.

I know I stated previously to steer clear of some 'rules of thumb' for your plan. I am sure you could have the court reporter read back to me (*A Few Good Men* reference) what I wrote. Please note these "rules" are merely meant to help you with this example by illustrating how much money you may need to generate a guaranteed payment. Your advisor will walk you through all the options available in the marketplace based on your situation but it is a good place to start.

The key is to realize that for Pears to fully cover their Needs, they will need to utilize their portfolio to generate the guarantees. The exact amount will be determined by interest rates and the marketplace at the time of purchase, so it will be helpful to have your advisor team run quotes for you.

In the example above, if this Pear household retires tomorrow and is short $1,150/month, then it would take around a quarter of a million dollars to provide the necessary level of income for life. If they were retiring five years from now, they could set aside almost 30% less money to provide a similar level of income. If the goal were to retire in 10 years, they would be looking at 45% less to reach that same level.

The amount of time between when you begin and when you need the income will dictate which instruments to choose. Whenever that may be, you will need enough money to purchase them.

The chart below illustrates the difference between investing for retirement and investing during retirement as a Pear. The focus during earning years is accumulating wealth, but in retirement it normally is to protect it. Pears were fine with a growth-oriented portfolio while getting a paycheck, but now need to focus on income. They were not concerned about the 2008 Financial Crisis because retirement was not imminent, but may now be nervous about the 2020 Pandemic Crisis if a retirement is planned soon. So, they prefer to not accept as much volatility in their portfolio.

They also used to be focused on deferring taxes by funding retirement accounts, but now that they will eventually stop funding them, they are interested in how to reduce taxes in retirement.

Mitigating Risks

	Investing for Retirement	Investing During Retirement
Investment Objectives:	Accumulation	Preserve Principal
Appreciation & Earnings:	Seek Growth	Seek Income
Risk:	Risk Based on Time Horizon	Seek Lower Risk
Taxes:	Defer Taxes	Save or Reduce Taxes

The biggest risk for Pears is cash flow and the rising cost of living, since their necessities are not covered by Social Security or pensions, and most guaranteed income payments do not keep pace with the rising cost of living.

In my office, I have magnet cards that I purchased years ago at the local post office. They belong to the Remember When ... A Nostalgic Look Back in Time series. I have seven cards, each representing a decade, ranging from 1940 to 2000. Each states the average cost for a given product at that time; for example, a new house cost $4,075 in 1941 and $78,220 in 1981. The average income rose from $9,357 per year in 1970 to $41,343 per year in 2000.

I remember my parents telling me when I was a kid that when they grew up in the 50s, milk was a dollar and gasoline was 25¢ a gallon. They also used to walk 5 miles (each way) to school every day too, but I digress.

Well, they were right (at least about the milk and gasoline). In 2000 a postage stamp was 33¢. Twenty years later we pay 50¢. This is a 52% increase over two decades. I could go on about the rising cost of living, but hopefully you get my point, which is this: **To continue your current standard of living, you must have an income stream that rises during your retirement because what you purchase will go up in price over time.**

It is for this reason that owning investments that have the potential to increase in value over time, such as stocks—whether in mutual, index, or individual form—is very important. Since the focus for Pears is to provide enough guaranteed income to meet Needs there is a risk of keeping pace with the rising cost of living. Many annuities offer the ability to add in certain cost of living increases each year. This provides added protection as you age, but in return the original monthly payment will be less and not realistic to cover a Pear's basic Needs.

There are no free lunches in life, and the same can be said for retirement planning. There are pros and cons to the decisions you will make, but before you can properly assess them, you must know what your purpose and end goals are. This may result in major decisions regarding when to retire, where to live, and what to spend for a Pear.

Chapter 7

Apples

If you have never tasted a bad apple, you
would not appreciate a good apple. You have
to experience life to understand life.

— Leon Brown

Apples are widest in the middle. Most of the people reading this book are Apples. They have the guaranteed income from pensions and Social Security to meet their Needs, so they can prioritize their income Wants while maintaining the proper level of risk tolerance. In fact, if someone were a Pear with enough wealth, once they have secured a guaranteed income stream, they would become an Apple and should shift their focus to covering their Wants. Apples should consider three different methods of distributing income from their portfolio.

Apples: Questions to Ask

LEGACY

·WANTS·

NEEDS

How will my risk comfort zone play a role in meeting my Wants?

How much will it take to meet my Wants?

Apples Retirement Worksheet

Income Source	C1 & C2 Live
Pension	$3,500
Pension	$0
SS@FRA	$2,750
SS@FRA	$1,500
Total	$7,850
Income Goal	C1 & C2 Live
Needs	$7,500
Surplus	+$350
Wants	$2,500
Shortfall	-$2,150

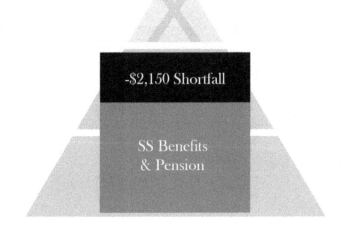

-$2,150 Shortfall

SS Benefits
& Pension

Here is an example of an Apple using the same C1 and C2. The difference is that the Needs are covered by guaranteed income sources, and the Wants are not. They need to be provided by distributions from their portfolio.

The Apples Retirement worksheet shows a $2,150/month shortfall in Wants. There are a few ways to cover this difference. The Apples may have enough wealth to cover their Wants by merely having some of the dividends from their portfolio distributed to them. This is one option and is further discussed below. The second option is considered a total return strategy. This method looks at the portfolio as a whole and is managed according to the comfort level of the investor. The final option (and most common) adopting a portfolio allocation strategy focused on separating investments according to the time until the monies are needed. This is called a bucket strategy.

Let's look at all three.

Dividend Stock Strategy

The benefit of a dividend strategy is that you do not have to touch the principal. It is a wonderful strategy. You would create this by selecting investments in solid companies with healthy balance sheets and sustainable income, and who pay dividends. The dividends are then used to cover this difference.

You could create a portfolio by selecting investments that pay dividends monthly or quarterly, depending on when you need the income. The risk with this strategy is what happens during a downturn when the value of those companies drops dramatically. Absent extreme shocks to the system, most companies continue to pay dividends, but it should be noted that dividend payments are not guaranteed and may be reduced or eliminated at any time by the company, even if they have decades of consistency.

This strategy is normally reserved for clients with a certain level of wealth, and there is some flexibility already built into the equation such that if principal distributions became necessary, it would be okay. The primary option is to just live off the income each year. So, in good years, you can spend more. In bad years, you tighten up the belt.

Dividend Stock Strategy

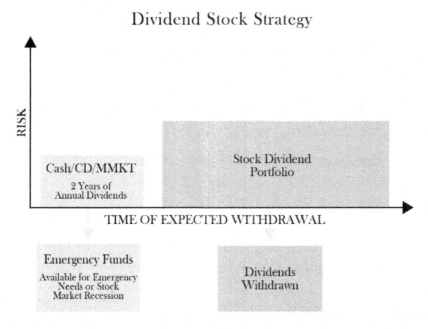

In other words, using the dividend strategy requires you to create a decent amount of wealth but in return frees the retiree from the concern of drawing from the principal of the portfolio. As long as the investor can be flexible during down years in which dividends may drop, they will be rewarded with the potential for a higher income (and greater spending levels) when the market rebounds. The flexibility during market drops would be provided by keeping two years of annual dividends in cash, such that if dividends are reduced you have that cash to cover the difference.

Let's say, for example, the U.S. stock market is paying a 2.5% dividend yield and you have a $1M portfolio. Your income alone will be $25k per year. You will owe ordinary income tax on this. For simplicity's sake, let's assume your marginal tax rate is 20%, bringing you to $20k per year of spendable income without selling any shares. If your budget shows a $1,500 per month deficit to cover your Wants—that's $18k per year—a dividend strategy could be an option.

From 1960 to 2019, the S&P 500 dividend yield has ranged from a low of 1.15% to a high of 5.57% and continues to depend on a variety of factors.[16] This is one of the reasons that I do not employ dividend strategies as often as I might like. It is due to the variability in yields and the realistic nature of humans to avoid having to drastically cut spending should yields drop. I also do not prefer to stretch for yields, as this could add unnecessary risk to a portfolio. However, these can be mitigated by holding cash to supplement your income during this period and through a diligent stock screening process to weed out companies that are too risky for a stock dividend model.

The other reason is that many retirees have an emotionally difficult time with stock market drops and "cannot bare to see the bear" when their portfolio drops 20% or more in a short period of time. There is a saying that the best laid plans mean nothing if not followed properly. It is important to "know thyself." If you can't handle the ride, do not buy the ticket. This strategy is not for you.

On the flip side, if you won't freak out during market declines, and can be flexible in your Want spending during these times, you will most likely end up with a greater level of income protection in your later years, as well as creating more terminal wealth. It is for this reason that the stock dividend strategy is nicely suited for the investor that can handle ups and downs in market valuations and adapt their income accordingly. It is also an ideal portfolio structure for a Strawberry because dividends can be reinvested for future generations.

Total Return Strategy

The total return strategy from my standpoint is just as it states: your portfolio is allocated to get a desired return to fit your income per your Wants. While the desired return could be 6%, your investments from year to year will be higher or lower. This strategy allocates them across stocks and bonds (and maybe some other asset classes) that would historically put you in range for the desired output needed to supplement your Wants.

Unlike the dividend strategy, in which no principal is redeemed, the total return strategy will need to sell shares over time because there will be down years that do not allow for the dividends to cover your Wants.

There have been many white papers written and studies performed in the financial planning world on what is a reasonable rate of withdrawal from your portfolio. At one point, there was something called the 4% rule, which suggested that if you took 4% per year from your portfolio, you would not run out of money. It took a few years, but this theory was tested, and it was determined that there are just too many variables that come into play, such as inflation, investment returns, economic cycles, and interest rates to be reliable. In recent years, it has been suggested that a 3% withdrawal rate is more realistic as a projection due to low interest rates and bond yields.

Success Rates for Total Return Strategies
Based on above Assumptions

Since the total return strategy is based on a certain withdrawal rate, and your portfolio will need to be constructed to fit your plan and comfort level, I thought it helpful to share with you the difference between withdrawal rates of portfolios with different levels of stocks.

The top portfolio illustrates 25% stocks, while the bottom illustrates 65% stocks. You will not notice much of a difference if there is a low cost of living adjustment (COLA) during retirement at 4% withdrawal rates or below. But, if inflation raises its ugly head, or you are withdrawing 4% or more per year, it will make a HUGE difference in your success.

The Portfolio Success Rates Chart shows that a 4% initial withdrawal rate for a conservative portfolio with 25% stocks has a 93% chance of lasting 35 years if COLA is 3% per year. However, if inflation goes up to 4%, then the success rate is 71%.

A 5% inflation rate in the conservative portfolio shows your success rate is only 46%!

Under a balanced portfolio with 65% stocks, the assumptions of 3%, 4%, and 5% inflation rates provide 98%, 96%, and 91% success rates respectively.

You may be reading this thinking a 5% cost of living is too high. If so, take those bell-bottoms from the 70s out of your closet back and know that the average inflation rate during that decade was 6.8%. All of the recent government spending, accommodative monetary policy with low interest rates suggest that rising inflation may be part of our future.

Portfolio Success Rates

Conservative Retirement Portfolio (25% Stock/75% Fixed Income) 15% Large-Cap Stock, 10% Small-Cap Stock, 55% Bonds, 20% Cash						
	Initial Withdrawal Rate					
	2%	3%	4%	5%	6%	7%
COLA	Historical Success Rate of Portfolio Lasting 35 Years					
0%	100%	100%	100%	100%	93%	64%
1%	100%	100%	100%	96%	71%	36%
2%	100%	100%	100%	82%	46%	24%
3%	100%	100%	93%	58%	33%	20%
4%	100%	100%	71%	36%	20%	13%
5%	100%	93%	46%	26%	13%	2%

Balanced Retirement Portfolio (65% Stock/35% Fixed Income) 40% Large-Cap Stock, 25% Small-Cap Stock, 25% Bonds, 10% Cash						
	Initial Withdrawal Rate					
	2%	3%	4%	5%	6%	7%
COLA	Historical Success Rate of Portfolio Lasting 35 Years					
0%	100%	100%	100%	98%	95%	91%
1%	100%	100%	100%	98%	95%	89%
2%	100%	100%	100%	95%	89%	86%
3%	100%	100%	98%	91%	87%	71%
4%	100%	100%	96%	89%	80%	55%
5%	100%	98%	91%	87%	64%	29%

Source: American Association of Individual Investors Journal, Jan 2016 - "The Mathematics of Retirement Portfolio" by Craig Israelsch

Being too conservative with a total return strategy may make you feel better early in retirement, but it gives you a higher probability of running out of money.

A good total return strategy will begin retirement with balanced stock exposure to limit the risk of a large market drop at the beginning, but as time goes on it will add more stocks to protect against the rising cost of living.

Another way of looking at this is the Rule of 300 (more aggressive) or the Rule of 400 (more conservative), depending on your risk comfort level. This allows you to take your monthly figure in your budget and multiply it by the rule you prefer. (I also included the rules for the annual figure if you are budgeting annually instead.)

Notice below how much in assets you should have in your portfolio to cover your Wants during your retirement based on a total return strategy.

Rule of 300 (4% Rule):
Take the monthly income need and multiply by 300.
  Current Example: $2,150 x 300 = $645,000
  $645,000 x 4% withdrawal rate = $25,800
  $25,800 / 12 = $2,150/month

Rule of 25 = Annual Expenses x 25 = Portfolio value needed
  $25,800/year x 25 = $645,000

Rule of 400 (3% Rule):
Take the monthly income need and multiply by 400.
  Current Example: $2,150 x 400 = $860,000
  $860,000 x 3% withdrawal rate = $25,800
  $25,800 / 12 = $2,150/month

Rule of 33 ⅓ = Annual Expenses x 33 = Portfolio value needed
  $25,800/year x 33 ⅓ = $860,000

As you can see from the examples above, the more conservative 3% withdrawal rate (Rule of 400) would require $860k to implement, while the 4% withdrawal (Rule of 300) would require $645k.

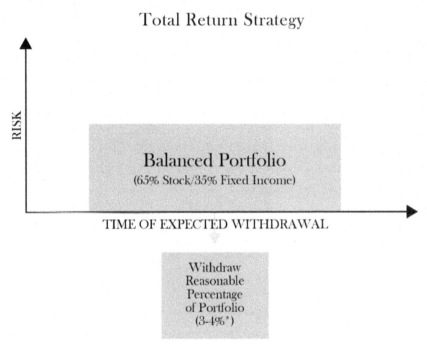

*Depending on a variety of variable market conditions. Consult with your advisor for steps appropriate for your personal situation.

What if in this example there are not enough investable assets to meet the Wants? Well, similar to a Pear, you will have to rethink your Wants and the cost to have them. If there is not enough gas in the tank, then you need to look at another form of travel or shorten the length of your trip.

Should you fall into this situation, I recommend you put your life on the table and start with your calendar. Get a red pen and look at your activities. Which ones cost the most to do? Which ones can you live without? Which Wants are a must keep?

Bucket Strategy

Apples could consider using a bucket strategy to distribute wanted income into time frames using assets that have varying degrees of risk. This is called time segmentation.

The bucket strategy is the most common retirement income strategy that I use with clients. It divides investment assets into different buckets depending on the time horizon for withdrawal and the client's risk tolerance. I think this is because it is easy to see and remember.

People tend to stay the course during declines because they are in solid shape, knowing that monies needed in the short term are invested differently. I find that this strategy allows retirees to sleep well at night.

The Bucket Strategy Overview chart shows how a bucket strategy works.

The first bucket is called Emergency Focus and should consist of cash and cash equivalents needed in the next 2 years. The second is Income Preservation and should consist of bonds and inflation-protected treasuries for distributions in years 3 – 7. The final bucket is called Growth and should hold equities that will not be needed for 8 years or more.

Growth means different things to different people. In this case, it absolutely must mean holding stocks. The benefit of the bucket strategy is that it allows you to hold stocks for the long term, and *you know you can follow through on that strategy during bad markets because you will not be touching those securities for a long time.* If you plan to fill your growth-oriented bucket with conservative investments, then you might as well just employ a conservative total return strategy. That said, it will require more money depending on your level of

Bucket Strategy Overview

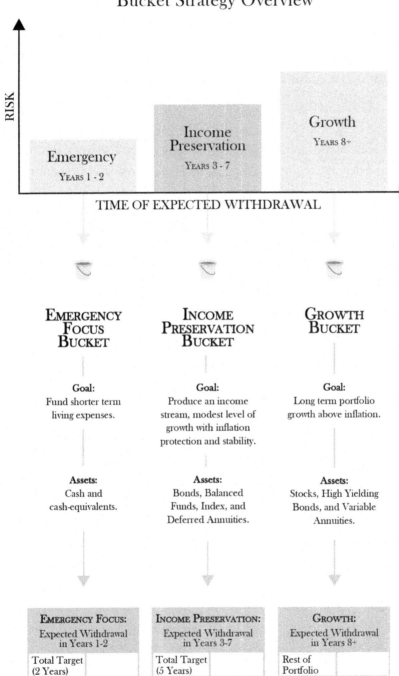

☜ Bucket Strategy 1

Rule of 300: Need $2,150/month = $645,000

YEAR 1 & 2	YEARS 3-7	YEARS 8 +
Cash/CD/Money Market $51,600	Bonds/Balanced Allocation $141,000	Stocks/Growth Allocation $452,400
$2,150/month	$2,350/month	$2,724/month

Separating your investment portfolio based on time until distribution.

Inflation assumption 3% per year. Annuity is an estimate for a single life with no COLA.

withdrawals to fit your income plan so it is prudent to review your probabilities of success with each strategy.

Let's continue to use our example with the Rule of 300 as a guide:

If there is a change in income requirements or risk tolerance, the buckets can be rebalanced.

As each year passes, your advisory team should review the buckets and make appropriate changes to ensure the plan is still in balance. Their job is to not just create the plan but to monitor it and make adjustments as necessary to fit the strategy. Your portfolio will move through time and, as the world changes, so should your portfolio—especially in the growth part of the bucket. As I'm writing this, Exxon Mobil just got kicked out of the Dow Jones Industrial Average. This is important considering it was part of the benchmark for 92 years, which is amazing when considering this index is comprised of only 30 companies. The point is that the world is not static, and unless you plan on becoming your own portfolio manager, you may desire to have a professional as part of your plan for navigating retirement.

TOP 10 S&P 500 COMPANIES
by Market Capitalization

	1980	1990	2000	2010	2020
1	IBM	IBM	General Electric	Exxon Mobil	Apple
2	AT&T	Exxon	Exxon Mobil	Apple	Microsoft
3	Exxon	General Electric	Pfizer	Microsoft	Amazon
4	Standard Oil of Indiana	Philip Morris	Citigroup	Berkshire Hathaway	Facebook
5	Schlumberger	Royal Dutch Petrol	Cisco Systems	General Electric	Alphabet Class A
6	Shell Oil	Bristol-Myers Squibb	Wal-mart	Wal-mart	Alphabet Class C
7	Mobil	Merck	Microsoft	Google	Johnson & Johnson
8	Standard Oil of California	Wal-mart	AIG	Chevron	Berkshire Hathaway
9	Atlantic Richfield	AT&T	Merck	IBM	Proctor & Gamble
10	General Electric	Coca-Cola	Intel	Proctor & Gamble	Visa
Total Market Cap	$236B	$437.5B	$2.75T	$2.22T	$7.51T
% Increase		85%	529%	-24%	238%

The top 2 names in 2020 were over 45% greater in market cap value than the top 10 in 2010.

Note: 2020 rankings as of 08/21/2020

https://etfdb.com/history-of-the-s-and-p-500
https://www.investopedia.com/top-10-s-and-p-500-stocks-by-index-weight-4843111

To further illustrate the concept of 'As the World Turns' (I was more of a Days of Our Lives kind of kid growing up but I digress), you will see Exxon Mobil shown on the S&P 500 from 20 years ago was number 2. Anyone remember Eastman Kodak or Xerox?

Because many of the decisions we make, financial and otherwise, are based on emotion, the bucket strategy is a good hedge against acting rashly when there is a sharp downturn in the market. Because short-term investments are in cash or other liquid securities, a market downturn is less worrisome because it only impacts the long-term buckets.

Even with that said, some of you may like the idea of using guaranteed income to cover not just your Needs but also some of your Wants. This is something that you can easily add to your plan, as shown below in the Strategy 2 visual below. The key is to determine your risk comfort level.

There are certainly trade-offs between using an investment-only strategy and adding a guaranteed annuity to supplement the investment strategy. The key is to follow whatever strategy you put in place. In other words, if you can't handle it when things get a little messy and would sell out of your equity investments during the next recession, then you should look at some options that will allow you to stay the course with the equity portion of your portfolio, as that is the long-term engine that will keep pace with the rising cost of goods.

For Apples, 100% guaranteed income may sound nice and feel good in the short term, and especially during bear markets, but in the long term you may limit the ability for your income to combat inflation. You also lose the flexibility of taking additional monies from your portfolio down the road to do something fun or give to a great cause.

In effect, it limits Apples flexibility when they put all their monies into a guaranteed annuity product, which is why we only show a hybrid approach There is an exception, though, if an Apple has substantial assets leftover after guaranteeing both Needs and Wants. This moves the Apple up to a Strawberry because now all Needs and Wants are fully covered AND there is a healthy investment portfolio leftover.

As to whether the investment or the hybrid approach is best for you, that depends on your comfort zone. It is a topic that your advisor should be spending a lot of time on to create the best plan with you.

What is the Role of My Risk Comfort Zone?

Investment Type	Annuities	Investments
Benefits	Guaranteed Income	Higher market upside
	Downside Protection	Inflationary protection
	Guaranteed Growth while delaying income	Flexibility
Trade-off	Less Flexibility	More Zig and Zag
	Reduced Inflation Hedge	Sequence of Returns Risk
	Lower growth	Income not guaranteed

It is their responsibility to know you and your investment biases and potential behaviors. It is one thing to say you can handle a 30% drop in your portfolio when you are working, but you will have a completely different perspective when you are no longer receiving a paycheck.

See the chart below for a bucket strategy for Apples combining investments and an annuity.

▽ Bucket Strategy 2

Rule of 300: Need $2,150/month = $645,000

Rule of 225: Use $225k to purchase $1k/month Guaranteed Income Annuity

YEAR 1 & 2	YEARS 3-7	YEARS 8 +
Cash/CD/Money Market $27,600	Bonds/Balanced Allocation $81,000	Stocks/Growth Allocation $311,400
$1,150/month	$1,350/month	$1,724/month
$1,000/month from Single Premium Immediate Annuity		

Inflation assumption 3% per year. Annuity is an estimate for a single life with no COLA.

The greatest risk for Apples is to allow fear to drive financial decisions and avoid huge investment losses early in retirement.

The order of our returns is not as important when we are accumulating money, but it is *very* important when we distribute it. This is known as sequence of returns. The following visual shows a 25-year history of returns for Portfolio A, and then flip flops the returns for Portfolio B, such that the last year is the first year, and so on. Portfolio A makes money early on and loses at the end, while Portfolio B does the opposite.

Does it make a difference? As my mother would say, "Is the Pope Catholic?" Oh, my goodness, yes!

This is because if we are selling investments that have dropped early on, we must sell more shares to get the money we desire, and it is harder to make up that loss. If we are taking out 3% per year, and we make 10%, this is not an issue; however, if we lose 10% (or more), it becomes a major issue.

How do you mitigate this risk? Employ the bucket strategy, because the money is coming from places where you have not lost during market declines due to your 2-year cash cushion.

	Average returns & asset allocation					Sequence of returns & product allocation			
	ACCUMULATION					**DISTRIBUTION**			
	Start with $100,000 and take no withdrawals for annual income.					Start with $691,527 and begin with a $35,000 /year distribution adjusted for 3% inflation.			

	PORTFOLIO A		PORTFOLIO B			PORTFOLIO A		PORTFOLIO B	
	Annual Return	Year-end Value	Annual Return	Year-end Value		Annual Return	Year-end Value	Annual Return	Year-end Value
41	29%	$129,000	-12%	$88,000	66	29%	$846,920	-12%	$577,744
42	18%	$152,220	-21%	$69,520	67	18%	$956,827	-21%	$427,938
43	25%	$190,275	-14%	$59,787	68	25%	$1,149,620	-14%	$336,094
44	-6%	$178,859	22%	$72,940	69	-6%	$1,044,692	22%	$363,375
45	15%	$205,687	10%	$80,234	70	15%	$1,156,094	10%	$356,381
46	8%	$222,142	4%	$83,444	71	8%	$1,204,761	4%	$328,438
47	27%	$282,121	11%	$92,623	72	27%	$1,476,970	11%	$318,178
48	-2%	$276,478	3%	$95,401	73	-2%	$1,405,246	3%	$283,386
49	15%	$317,950	-3%	$92,539	74	15%	$1,565,046	-3%	$231,877
50	19%	$378,360	21%	$111,973	75	19%	$1,808,061	21%	$225,315
51	33%	$503,219	17%	$131,008	76	33%	$2,342,161	17%	$208,585
52	11%	$558,574	5%	$137,558	77	11%	$2,546,022	5%	$168,143
53	-10%	$502,716	-10%	$123,802	78	-10%	$2,246,508	-10%	$106,418
54	5%	$527,852	11%	$137,421	79	5%	$2,304,865	11%	$61,071
55	17%	$614,587	33%	$182,769	80	17%	$2,634,751	33%	$10,813
56	21%	$747,280	19%	$217,496	81	21%	$3,122,069	19%	$0
57	-3%	$724,862	15%	$250,120	82	-3%	$2,973,927	15%	$0
58	3%	$746,608	-2%	$245,118	83	3%	$3,003,560	-2%	$0
59	11%	$828,734	27%	$311,299	84	11%	$3,267,812	27%	$0
60	4%	$861,884	8%	$336,203	85	4%	$3,334,697	8%	$0
61	10%	$948,072	15%	$386,634	86	10%	$3,598,631	15%	$0
62	22%	$1,156,648	-6%	$363,436	87	22%	$4,310,895	-6%	$0
63	-14%	$994,717	25%	$454,295	88	-14%	$3,649,695	25%	$0
64	-21%	$785,827	18%	$536,068	89	-21%	$2,828,690	18%	$0
65	-12%	$691,527	29%	$691,527	90	-12%	$2,426,637	29%	$0

MARKET CYCLE IMPACT
• Losses in early years of distribution may prevent receiving income for life
• Considering only average rates of return over a long period can be misleading
• Professional financial management can help minimize risk

This example is hypothetical and does not represent any actual investment.

NOTE:
Randomly chosen whole number returns. The distribution increases at 3% per year from the original $35,000. It is assumed to be taken at the beginning of the year before the yearly return is calculated.

Chapter 8

Strawberries

We make a living by what we get.
We make a life by what we give.

— Winston Churchill

Strawberries are our most well-rounded fruits. They have enough guaranteed income to cover their Needs and their Wants without touching their other assets, so they can now prioritize leaving behind a Legacy by leveraging tax-efficient vehicles like life insurance.

As noted previously, you can only be one fruit at a time, but your fruit can change based on your situation. For example, under the Apple Bucket strategy #2, an immediate annuity was purchased so that the investment portfolio did not have to withdrawal as much. This provided a more conservative scenario for the retiree since less monies were needed from the investment portfolio. In return for potentially less wealth down the road, the retiree prefers more guaranteed income. Now, if the retiree had enough assets to purchase an income stream for life that covered both Needs and Wants, he or she would now become a Strawberry. See how this works? Alternatively, that same retiree who has enough assets may prefer the stock dividend approach instead. There are many ways to slice an Apple (excuse the pun but I couldn't help myself).

The Strawberries I tend to work with fit into this category due to their pensions provided to them for their years of service, whether it be military, federal, or in the corporate world. In addition, the social security income stream merely adds to this guaranteed level of income, many times with a cost of living adjustment, that cannot be outlived. It then leads to the conversation of leaving a Legacy. I always say that to give is to receive, and there are many ways to give that do not require money. A mere smile costs nothing but can change someone's day. Giving up your time through volunteer work is another gift of energy that is exponential. I advise both and would suggest you get back ten-fold what you give, but this conversation is about our financial Legacy.

Choosing tax-efficient vehicles is important because if *you* don't spend your money, who will? That is not a rhetorical question, by the way. The answer is: your family or the government, via taxation.

As of 2020, a federal estate tax applies only if the deceased's assets total $11.58M or more. A dozen states have their own estate taxes, and six have inheritance taxes. Both have lower thresholds than the federal estate tax. Taxes are only assessed on the value of the estate or inheritance that is over the threshold level, and surviving spouses are typically exempt from these taxes regardless of the value of the estate or the inheritance.

Strawberries need to focus on strategies that will ensure that their money goes where they want it to go.

The greatest risks for Strawberries are taxes and leaving money behind with no plan to distribute it.

Strawberries Retirement Worksheet

Income Source	C1 & C2 Live
Pension	$6,500
Pension	$0
SS@FRA	$2,750
SS@FRA	$1,500
Total	$10,750
Income Goal	C1 & C2 Live
Needs	$7,500
Surplus	+$3,250
Wants	$2,500
Surplus	+750

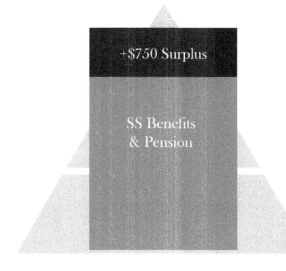

+$750 Surplus

SS Benefits
& Pension

Legacy Planning

Income Source	C1 & C2 Live	C1 Passes	C2 Passes
Pension	$6,500	$3,250	$6,500
Pension	$0	$0	$0
SS@FRA	$2,750	$0	$2,750
SS@FRA	$1,500	$2,750	$0
Total	$10,750	$6,000	$9,250
Income Goal	C1 & C2 Live	C1 Passes	C2 Passes
Needs	$7,500	$6,375	$6,375
Surplus/Shortfall	+$3,250	-$375	+$2,875
Wants	$2,500	$2,125	$2,125
Surplus/Shortfall	+$750	-$2,500	+$750

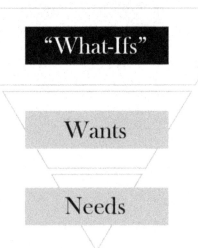

Strawberries have different concerns and we will cover a few strategies that should be considered for Legacy planning.

Legacy Strategy #1 - Roth IRA Conversion

If you have a traditional IRA, you may consider a Roth conversion. A conversion allows investors to move money from a traditional IRA, pay taxes on it at the ordinary federal income tax rates, and put it into a Roth, where it will grow tax-free. Future withdrawals can be taken tax-free as long as you meet the requirements.

Roth conversions allow you to pay taxes today (ideally to the top of your tax bracket to avoid increasing your marginal tax rate) so that you do not have to pay them in the future. Yes, you read that correctly. There is a way to pay in advance on our retirement accounts now if we think taxes will be higher in the future. Quick history check—the highest marginal tax rate in 1960 was 91%.

Why do a conversion? Because the odds are high that tax rates in the future will be higher than they are currently as well as your account values. Would you rather pay tax on an ant hill or a mountain? It is especially advantageous to do a Roth Conversion in a down market. To convert, you pay taxes on the fair market value of the taxable portion of the IRA. So, if you have an IRA invested in stock X, which is down 40%, and you convert it to a Roth, you pay taxes on the fair value. This means that the cost of converting 100 shares of stock x is less when the share price is temporarily down. Should stock x revert to its price prior to conversion, you have the same number of shares, but those shares are now in a tax-free account and you paid a reduced cost for that to happen. During the COVID crisis and resulting market drop, we did a lot of Roth conversions for precisely the reasons mentioned above. When the market recovered all of those shares were now in a tax-free bucket paid for at a lower cost.

Think about it this way: If you look at the balance of your traditional IRA, 401k, 403b, or 457, you should note that not all those monies are yours. In reality, Uncle Sam gets his cut first. Imagine you and I start a business together. Our partnership agreement states that upon dissolution, I get to decide how much I get first, and you get what's leftover. In essence, if all your monies are in traditional accounts, the IRS decides how much they take before your get your piece via your marginal tax rate.

Now, if you think that tax rates in our country will remain the same throughout your retirement, then I would like to sell you my old cassette player. History suggests that the income taxes we pay will change over time based on political, social, and economic environments. We delve into this later in the book, but the point is that planning ahead can give you greater control over your assets.

Roth conversions allow you to pay taxes today (ideally to the top of your tax bracket to avoid increasing your marginal tax rate) so that you do not have to pay them in the future. Yes, you read that correctly. There is a way to pay taxes on our retirement accounts now if we think they will be higher in the future.

In our example below we have a family making $120,000 per year, which puts them in the 22% tax bracket. The top of the 22% bracket in 2020 is $171,050. So, if we converted $51,050 of tax-deferred dollars today, we could move these dollars into the tax-free bucket without increasing our marginal rate.

Implementing this strategy today could play a big role in retirement for those whose income will consist of more than just pensions and Social Security (taxable income streams you cannot avoid). By doing some planning now, you will allow your monies to grow without concern of required minimum distributions at age 72 *and* never be taxed again on these dollars.

It should be noted that your advisory team will know when tax rates change and will update the strategy to fit the current tax structure.

Legacy Strategy 1

Roth Coversion(s):
- Can be done in a lump sum or over time
- Conversions to top of marginal Tax Bracket allow for tax-free growth moving forward
- Down Market opportunity

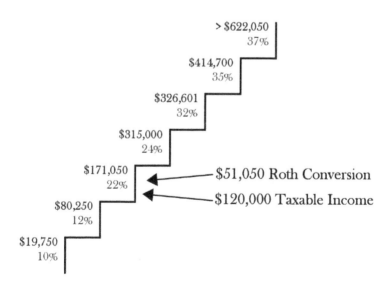

Traditional IRA account owners should consider the tax ramifications, age, and income restrictions in regards to executing a conversion from a Traditional IRA to a Roth IRA. The converted amount is generally subject to income taxation.

Legacy Strategy #2 – Purchase a life policy from your RMD

Another strategy for Strawberries is to leverage the RMD from your IRA by purchasing a life insurance policy. Essentially, you could do this a few ways but two are shown in the visual below. To the left side you just take the RMD (required minimum distributions) from your IRA to pay the premiums. The most recent law states that the calendar year in which you turn age 72 you must start withdrawing from your tax-deferred accounts (Traditional IRA, 401k, 457, 403(b), TSP, etc.). The amount withdrawn is based on a figure your advisor will calculate for you every year using your prior year-end balance and an IRS life expectancy table. To the right side of the chart, the idea would be to purchase a single premium immediate annuity using your IRA. This would provide a guaranteed income stream (as discussed above for Pears and Apples) over your lifetime. Since Strawberries do not need the income and are focused on providing a Legacy, this guaranteed income stream provided by the annuity would be used to purchase a life insurance policy.

Both options leverage your estate and can add value to it through the income-tax-free death benefit. Life Couples would purchase a second-to-die policy, while a single premium life policy would be purchased otherwise. Look at how much that $20k/year premium turns into instantly via life insurance! It can be a very effective tool in many estate plans.

Legacy Strategy 2

IRA Balance
$512,000

A RMD

B PURCHASE SINGLE PREMIUM ANNUITY

$20,000/year
Purchase Life Insurance Policy
Income Tax-Free Benefit to Heirs

SINGLE MALE	SINGLE FEMALE	2ND TO DIE
$562,000	**$564,000**	**$925,000**
Tax-Free Death Benefit	Tax-Free Death Benefit	Tax-Free Death Benefit

A Received Minimum Distribution.
For a male or female age 72 with a year-end balance prior to turning 72 of $512,000 would be exactly $20,000.

B Using the Rule of 225.
Gross income for Life would be $27,306/year. Taxes would be owed on this income. This is a hypothetical to illustrate a potential strategy. Please consult with your financial advisor for actual illustrations appropriate for your situation.

Legacy Strategy #3 – Qualified Charitable Distributions

The third Legacy strategy would be to take advantage of the tax code by doing a QDC, or qualified charitable distribution. This is very simple: once you hit the RMD age, you can take your RMD, give it directly to charity and will not be taxed on the distribution.

Think about it this way, assume your left pocket is taxable and your right pocket is tax-free. Which pocket do you want to use to take from your IRA? Of course, your right pocket. However, what many people tend to do is give to charity by writing a check from their bank account. This bank account is funded from their RMD distribution coming from their left pocket. Instead, have your IRA account write the check to charity directly and save the tax.

Legacy Strategy 3

Use Required Minimum Distribution to give to Charity:
- RMD Payments directly to charity are tax-free
- Up to $100k of distributions per year
- Can be set up as a third party payee from IRA to the charitable organization
- Instant tax savings

Legacy Strategy #4 – Charitable Trusts

The final Legacy strategy we will discuss in this book is the use of charitable trusts. There are a variety of trusts and many things to consider when implementing this strategy. This is yet another reason you should discuss your situation with your tax, financial, and legal professionals. Setting up a trust results in choosing a trustee. This trustee could be a family member, professional, or corporate trustee. It is important to understand the differences. I've learned over the years each situation is different, but the end result tends to be an undesired outcome without the guidance of financial and legal professionals if considering this option.

For purposes of this book, it is important to know that a Strawberry has the ability to setup a trust that provides charitable intent and a tax deduction. The 501c(3) organization can either receive the money at the end of the trust's term or the donor's life (remainder trust) or as an income stream during it (lead trust). In both cases, the donor has the potential for tax savings, so the combination of giving to charity and receiving a tax benefit is valuable to the Legacy-minded retiree. The trust can be setup to have fixed payments (annuity trust) or revalued each year for variable income streams (unitrust).

Currently the low interest rates environment benefits the use of the charitable lead trusts because it results in a higher present value gift to the charity for tax purposes. It should also be noted that for Strawberries looking to conserve on taxes due to their heirs and estate upon death, the use of a grantor-retained trust can be an effective strategy. For Strawberries with highly appreciated stock or other assets, the use of a charitable trust can be a very effective estate planning tool that would otherwise limit your ability to do much with the asset without having a large tax bill.

Legacy Strategy 4

Charitable Remainder Trusts 'CRT'

Donor Assets
'Grantor'

CRT

Income   Remainder

Grantor   Charity

Income Tax
Deduction

Charitable Lead Trusts 'CLT'

Donor Assets

CRT

Income   Remainder

Charity   Beneficiaries

Income Tax
Deduction

See Legacy Strategy 4 to see the basic options for how charitable trusts operate

Benefits of CRT:

– Diversification of highly appreciated assets without triggering large taxes
– Opportunity to receive income during lifetime to use for other gifting purposes
– Potential to receive an immediate income tax deduction
– Ability to benefit to charity of your choice

Benefits of CLT:

– Diversification of highly appreciated assets without triggering large taxes
– Opportunity to provide a charity an annual income stream for a period of time
– Potential to receive an income or estate tax deduction depending on type of trust
– Ability to reduce overall estate taxes
– With interest rates so low, this is a very attractive option

It should also be noted that for Strawberries looking to conserve on inheritance or estate taxes upon death, the use of a grantor-retained trust can be an effective strategy. Essentially it is a way to distribute monies down the family tree by freezing the value of the trust assets while transferring any appreciation to the next generation, thereby potentially saving gift or estate tax.

Part III

TAKING CONTROL

*Incredible change happens in your life when you
decide to take control of what you do have power over,
instead of craving control over what you don't.*

– Anonymous

When it comes to our retirement funds, there are things we can control completely, things over which we have some control, and some over which we have no control.

The Risks

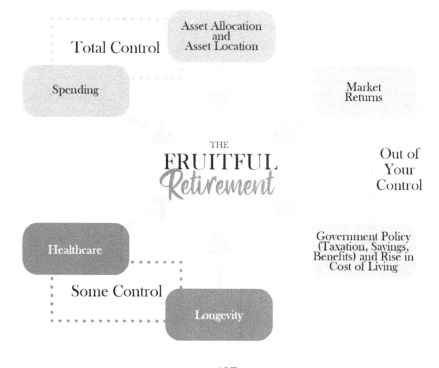

Total Control: Spending, Asset Allocation, Asset Location

Spending – The Go-Go years, the Slow-Go years, & the No-Go years

Retirement Aging Process

Go-Go Years → Slow-Go Years → No-Go Years

Spending does tend to decrease during retirement but by how much is debatable.[17] One study claims that real costs (i.e., inflation-adjusted) fall by 15% every 5 years. This means that in 20 years, people in their 70s could be spending less than half of what they were spending in their late 50s. Another study disputes these findings, claiming that there is an inflation-adjusted drop of just 1% per year, suggesting a 22% decline in spending over a 10-year period.

At what age you retire is a big determinant in how much you spend. The younger you are when you retire, the more similar your post-retirement spending will be to your pre-retirement spending—sometimes even outpacing it for the first decade or so. Many young retirees choose to do a lot of traveling, do not immediately downsize their home, and may have one or more children still in college, so their expenses don't drop off right away.

The budget you completed above as part of The Fruitful Retirement process should give you an idea of what your spending will be early on and how you will pay for it. As you think about spending over the next three decades, ask yourself this question: Do I know anyone over age 80, and if so, do they spend more or less money now than when they were in their 60s?

Most likely, the answer will only be yes if there are significant healthcare expenses. Otherwise, from years of experience with clients, I have noticed that the spending goes down.

I remember years ago when I was at local Rotary meeting. One of the elder Rotarians at the lunch table, who happened to be in his 80s at the time, mentioned to me that when he was younger, he loved to travel the world. Now, he said, it was far easier on him to see the world on the Discovery Channel. I think there is some truth to that based on how I see people live during their retirement years.

Every client I have ever worked with on retirement planning asks the same question at some point: Will the money eventually run out?

If I know the rate of return for your portfolio, how long you will live, how much you will spend, what the cost of living increases will be for the products and services you consume, whether you will have any expensive major health issues, and what additional familial or charitable considerations come into play, I can give you an accurate answer. But I don't know those things. I *can't* know those things. And neither can you, or anyone else, because none of us has a crystal ball.

But that does not mean we throw up our hands and hope for the best. It is not like we are working with no data at all. The reality is most of retirement income planning has to do with looking at the present and projecting out estimates based on our current and expected fiscal situation. Again, one of the most important tasks to complete when planning for retirement is to create your own budget.

The budget is going to change over time for the reasons we discussed above. Your activities will determine those changes. It is why we spent so much time at the beginning of this book discussing how you will be spending your time during retirement.

Asset Allocation

A key step in retirement planning is determining your time horizon—that is, how many years in the future you plan to retire. This number will be a key determinate in the allocation of your portfolio. The farther your horizon, the more risk you can afford to take in your portfolio.

Your returns need to outpace inflation to maintain the purchasing power of your money over the course of your retirement. Inflation is basically the rising cost of goods and services. Depending on the good or service, inflation will be different. Historically, the average rate of inflation is around 3%. That sounds like a small number, but at that rate, prices will double every 24 years.

Asset allocation is nothing more than a way of saying "Don't put all of your eggs in one basket" when it comes to investing. Having all your assets in cash is ludicrous because cash pays you nothing and it costs more to live every year. You would be losing money every year to inflation. Conversely, having all your money in stocks when you need to start withdrawing from your portfolio may not make sense if you do not have enough income from pensions, an adequate savings balance, or the ability to generate enough income from the portfolio to cover your Needs.

More formally, asset allocation is a systematic approach to diversification that can help you determine the most efficient mix of assets based on your risk tolerance and time horizon.

Asset allocation seeks to manage risk by diversifying your portfolio between the major asset classes, including stocks, bonds, and cash alternatives. Every asset class has a different level of risk and potential return. At any given time, one asset category may be increasing in value while another may be decreasing in value. Proper asset allocation manages risk but cannot guarantee profits or protect against loss. If the value of one asset class in your portfolio drops, the other asset classes in your portfolio can help soften the blow.

Asset allocation can help you ride out market fluctuations and protect your portfolio from a major loss in any one asset class. But it is important to understand the risk/reward trade-off. Generally, the greater the potential return of an investment, the greater the risk.

This means your portfolio should take into account your level of risk tolerance. Generally, you should not place all your assets in those categories that have the highest potential for gain if you are nervous about the prospect of a loss. But you don't want to err too much on the side of caution either and only invest in assets that have the lowest level of risk. Why? Because your portfolio may not give you the kind of returns you need to meet your financial goals.

Your time horizon also plays a part in your asset allocation strategy. Time horizon means how long until you need your money that has been allocated for a specific goal. When crafting your portfolio, ask yourself what you want to accomplish with your investments. Do you want to buy a home or a car soon? Would you like to be able to pay for your children's college education? What do you want your retirement to look like? These things all have different time horizons.

The shorter your time horizon, *the less zig and zag* you want to take with the money dedicated to the goal you are trying to achieve. If you are saving for a down payment on a home and you want to buy within the next five years, you want that money in a low-volatile investment. On the other hand, if you are saving for retirement that is decades in the future, you can invest for greater growth potential, which involves greater chance of the portfolio going up and down. This is somewhat mitigated by the long-time horizon because that money has plenty of time to ride out the rollercoasters of the market. If you are 60 and have a life expectancy of 84 years, a certain part of your portfolio will not be used for quite some time. This is an important part of retirement planning.

Whichever asset allocation strategy you decide on, it is important that you remember there is no such thing as a one-size-fits-all scenario. Your specific situation calls for a specific approach that you are comfortable with and that will help you meet your investing goals.

Asset location is a strategy employed to minimize taxes by taking advantage of the fact that different kinds of investments are treated differently under the tax code. An investor uses this strategy to determine which securities should be held in tax-deferred accounts and which should be held in taxable accounts to maximize after-tax returns.

To benefit from an asset location strategy, you need to have investments in both taxable and tax-deferred accounts. An investor who splits their assets between the two types of accounts and with similar asset mixes will see the greatest benefit.

A typical balanced portfolio might consist of 60% stocks/40% fixed income and contain investments in taxable and tax-deferred accounts.

While an investor's overall portfolio should be balanced, it does not mean that each account needs to have the same asset mix. Using the same asset allocation in each account overlooks the tax benefit of strategically placing securities in the kind of account that will result in the best after-tax return. How a security is taxed should determine where you locate it.

Asset location is not meant to replace asset allocation. You must first determine the proper asset mix for your portfolio, and then you can determine the best location for those assets to minimize tax drag.

Optimal asset location depends on a variety of things, including investor profile, current tax laws, time horizon, and the tax and return characteristics of the underlying securities. But there are some general principles we can use to determine the types of investments that are best suited to each kind of account.

Taxable Accounts

Tax-friendly stocks are best located in taxable accounts because of the lower capital gains, tax rates on dividends, and the ability to defer gains. More volatile investments should be in taxable accounts because of the opportunity to defer taxes and to capture tax losses on investments that are not performing and are sold at a recognized loss. Index funds, ETFs, and tax-free or tax-deferred bonds should also be held in taxable accounts.

Tax-Deferred Accounts

Taxable bonds, REITs, and related mutual funds should be located in tax-deferred accounts, as should mutual funds that frequently generate capital gains distributions.

Some Control: Healthcare, Quality of Life

Taxes

None of us can predict the future—well, not exactly—which is what it would take to eliminate your tax burden during retirement. Looking back, we can see how dramatically tax laws have changed over the years. In fact, when JFK was president, the highest marginal tax bracket was 90%! With our country's current fiscal position, it is not unrealistic to assume higher taxes down the road. So, while we cannot anticipate every tax-related variable, with some advance planning we can build in some flexibility to work with whatever the tax policies may be during our retirement.

You don't have to wait until retirement to lay the groundwork for minimizing your taxes. Having money in both tax-deferred (401k, IRA), tax-free (Roth IRA), and taxable accounts (joint/brokerage) provides flexibility to decide which account to distribute from. This decision will be determined by your income situation and the tax laws at the time.

You can accomplish this by contributing to either a traditional or Roth 401k at work, or in your own traditional or Roth IRA. The other option is to transfer money from your traditional IRA to your Roth IRA. This is called a conversion, if you recall from our discussion earlier, and allows you to pay the tax at today's tax rate and never have to pay income tax again on these monies.

Another way to save on taxes entails bunching up your charitable deductions in one year (to itemize) and take the standard deduction the next. You could also use any RMDs (required minimum distributions) to go directly to a charitable institution. These distributions from your IRA/401k will not be taxed.

Healthcare

Americans spend a fortune on healthcare and the amount continues to climb quickly and astronomically.

> The average American household spent almost $5,000 per person on health care in 2018. That's a 101% increase from the roughly $2,500 per person that Americans spent in 1984, according to an analysis of the Bureau of Labor Statistics Consumer Expenditures Survey. To make accurate comparisons, all dollar amounts were adjusted for inflation.[18]

While we cannot completely control the spiraling cost of healthcare, there are some things we can do to mitigate its impact.

Save on Medication

A generic medication typically costs 80 to 85% less than the name-brand version. The active ingredients are the same in generic and name-brand drugs; ask your provider to prescribe the generic version of a medication for you whenever possible. If there is no generic version (drug patents last for 20 years, so no generic version may be produced during that time) ask your provider if there is a different, less expensive drug that treats your condition.

Get the Most from Your Benefits

Since most of us are paying a fortune for health insurance, be sure to take advantage of it as much as possible. Many insurance policies cover preventative screenings, yearly wellness visits, and vaccines with no co-pay. Get routine health screenings that can help spot potential problems early, before they become bigger problems that are harder and more expensive to treat. If you have a chronic health condition like diabetes or asthma, ask if your insurer offers case managers who can help coordinate your care. Make use of any free or discounted services they offer like gym memberships or weight loss programs.

Use Urgent Care When Appropriate

Going to an urgent care center is cheaper and faster than being treated in the emergency room. Of course, there are some instances when the emergency room is the necessary option, but urgent cares are open later than a doctor's office. If your problem can't wait until the next day and isn't life threatening, urgent care will save time and money.

Opt for Outpatient

If you need a procedure or minor surgery, ask if there is an outpatient clinic that can accommodate you. These facilities are cheaper than having the same treatment in a hospital.

Private Testing Services

The costs of blood work, MRIs, CT scans, and the like are astronomical when performed by major healthcare networks. If you look, you will find local businesses and clinics that provide the same professional testing services at a fraction of the cost.

Choose In-Network Providers, Hospitals, and Facilities

When a provider or entity is in-network, it means they have a contractual agreement with your insurance company to charge you at lower rates than out-of-network providers will. Your insurance carrier can provide you with a list of in-network service providers.

Choose the Correct Plan

The insurance plan you choose should be dictated by the overall health of you and your family. If anyone has a chronic condition that requires a substantial amount of medical care and prescription medications, a plan with a higher premium but lower deductible may be more cost-effective than a plan with a lower monthly premium and a higher deductible.

Use a Health Care Savings Account (HSA) or Flexible Spending Account (FSA)

Some employers offer these accounts to help employees with the cost of health care expenses. They are accounts that let you set aside pre-tax money to pay for qualified health-related expenses like copays and prescription costs. There are certain restrictions as far as the type of plan you must have (high deductible) to be able to have these accounts, as well as annual funding limits.

The money in an HSA can be invested, rolls over each year, and can be transferred if you change jobs. The money in an FSA, however, cannot be invested. You must use it or lose it, usually within a calendar year, and it cannot be transferred when changing jobs. If your company offers an HSA, it is like a Roth IRA on steroids. You get to invest and get a tax deduction, let it grow tax-deferred, and if used for health expenses, redeem it tax-free. What a great deal! The IRS does not offer a free lunch very often, but this is one of those times you should go to the buffet.

Quality of Life

Quality of life and money are very similar. We all know that we need to avoid debt, save money, and invest. We all know that eating vegetables, regular exercise, and quality sleep are important. All these things are simple, but they are not always easy.

Quality of life is very different from life span. Modern medicine can keep us alive for a long time in the face of a lot medical challenges: diabetes, heart attack, stroke, cancer, even brain death. But, in my opinion, and I'm sure many of you reading this will agree, I would rather live fewer years free of debilitating medical issues than live for many years suffering.

Everyone will have a different definition of quality of life, but there are some aspects we probably all agree on. A good quality of life means being free of aches and pains, not relying on long-term medications or therapies, being able to exercise, having a full range of movement, and possessing a sharp mind.

We don't have total control over our quality of life, but we have a lot—even those of us who have illness and disease in our family history. Genetics loads the gun, but environment pulls the trigger.

> The genetics you were born with are pretty much fixed but do not necessarily control how you will live. Like a light switch, genes are either on or off. Think of the millions upon millions of genes in your genetic structure as gates, open or closed, that direct your life force one direction or another. Your lifestyle and diet control many of these gates and can open or close them guiding your body's mechanisms toward health or disease. The gates are controlled by you and your lifestyle. You control your life.[19]

What is considered healthy varies greatly. Vegan or paleo? Running or yoga? Dairy or nut milks? Keto or low fat? You get the idea. While we may not all agree on every aspect of what is healthy, we can agree on a few key things that will help protect your quality of life. And the better your quality of life, the less expensive your medical costs will be and the more you will be able to do the things you want to do during your retirement.

Keep Your Weight Under Control
Before you've retired is the perfect time to evaluate your health. When you are still working, you may have employer-sponsored health insurance that covers more than Medicare will, and knowing ahead of time that you have health issues may color your retirement planning decisions.

Schedule a checkup and the preventative exams recommended for those in your age group. Work with you providers to create a plan that will help you maintain or improve your health.

Obesity comes with an increased risk for a slew of associated illnesses and diseases, all of which are very expensive to treat, including type 2 diabetes, joint problems, and some types of cancer, all of which greatly impact the quality of life. Staying at or getting down to a healthy weight for your gender and height is one of the best things you can do to protect your health, wealth, and retirement plans.

Perhaps nothing in the realm of health is as controversial as what constitutes a healthy diet, but again, I am sure we can agree on some basics. Eat a lot of vegetables and a little fruit. Eat an adequate amount of protein and increase it as you age. As we age, our risk of muscle loss increases, as I am noticing with my 'Dad-bod' coming into its own! Getting plenty of protein (and weight-bearing exercise) can help reduce the risk of this muscle loss. Drink plenty of water, as it nourishes our body.

Get Moving

Exercise is not limited to running or lifting weights in a gym. Anything that gets you moving is exercise: walking, hiking, kayaking, yoga, tennis, martial arts, dancing, hockey, roller-blading. The list goes on.

And there are "non-exercise" activities that, while not exactly exercise, still get us off the couch and have health benefits. I'm talking about things like gardening, cleaning, yard work, and DIY home projects. If you do not currently have an exercise activity you like and regularly participate in, find one, try out different forms of exercise until you come across one you enjoy. Because when you enjoy doing something, you will be more likely to do it regularly.

Curb Your Vices

There is nothing wrong with having an occasional drink. In fact, I'm an outgoing guy and enjoy this aspect of being social. It even seems to have health benefits, especially if your drink of choice is red wine. Overdoing the drinking can have serious health (and social) consequences. If you are a smoker, talk to your doctor about a plan for quitting. There is more help available than ever: prescription medications, nicotine patches, and gum—even acupuncture and hypnosis.

Out of Your Control: Market Returns, Government Policy, Cost of Living

I saw a sign that stated: "I've learned that when you try to control everything, you enjoy nothing." Part of taking control is understanding which areas you can influence through your behavior and decision-making and which areas you cannot.

Market Returns

While none of us can control market returns, you can control your allocation. We discussed this above. This helps to insulate your portfolio from the inevitable dips in the market during the long-term permanent advances that occur. As you head toward and enter retirement, your strategy shifts from accumulating assets to protecting the assets you have accumulated. To do this, it is necessary to make your overall portfolio allocation more conservative leading up to retirement to mitigate a negative market return early. Studies have shown that as you age, it is beneficial to add stocks help combat the rising costs of living. We discuss the various strategies for allocating your portfolio later in this book.

Government Policy and Taxes

If someone had told me at the end of 2019 that within the first quarter of 2020 there would be a shutdown of economic activity imposed by the government, I would have thought that person was crazy. Well, the Coronavirus pandemic has done just that, and going through this I think it is a little easier to understand why we as investors have little short-term control over market returns. There are too many factors (social, economic, political, climatic) that lie beyond our power to accurately predict what income or estate tax rates will be in 10, 20, or 30 years.

Social Security Benefits – When to take them and will they be there?

This is one of the more frequent questions I get asked: When should I take Social Security? Social Security is basically longevity insurance. So, similar to the question of how much and what type of life insurance should you own, if you tell me when you (and your spouse) will die, how much the cost of your spending will rise over your lifetime, and how much your portfolio will return during that time, then I can calculate a very realistic figure for you. The reality is nobody knows exactly what the answers are to those three questions, so we use certain assumptions to generate our recommendations. The decision as to when to collect Social Security, from my perspective, is as much emotional as it is financial.

Most Americans will rely on Social Security for part of their retirement income, so deciding when to start collecting the benefit is a key part of retirement planning. The age at which you start receiving benefits will partly determine how much money you get each month and, the longer you wait, the more you get. When to take Social Security depends on a number of things, including:

- Whether you will work between the age of 62 and your full retirement age
- Your life expectancy
- Your marital status

If you are not at full retirement age as defined by Social Security (66 or 67 for most people) and are still working, it most likely won't make sense to start receiving benefits because if you make more than the Social Security earning limit, the benefit you receive will be reduced. Once you've reached full retirement age, your benefits will not be reduced no matter how much other income you earn, although your benefits may be taxed.

If you live to your standard life expectancy, you will receive almost the same amount of Social Security benefit whether you take it early or wait until later. No one knows how long they will live, but the Social Security Administration has a life expectancy calculator[20] that can at least give you a ballpark figure to work with. Normally I tell clients if you don't need the income then consider not taking it until either FRA (Full Retirement Age) or age 70. There is no point to wait until age age 70, but for every year you wait from FRA until age 70 your social security income amount will increase between 7-8%, so it must be considered.

If you have a medical condition or a family history of life-shortening medical conditions, it may be advisable for you to take Social Security early.

The future of Social Security is another of those things we would need a crystal ball to predict. We do have some data to work with though, and at the moment it is not promising. But the good news is that it can be resolved.

According to the 2019 annual report of the Social Security Board of Trustees, the trust funds that disburse retirement, disability and other Social Security benefits will be depleted by 2035. That does not mean Social Security will no longer be around; it means the system will exhaust its cash reserves and will be able to pay out only what it takes in year-to-year in Social Security taxes. If this comes to pass, Social Security would be able to pay about 80 percent of the benefits to which retired and disabled workers are entitled.[21]

So how should Social Security fit into your retirement plans?

I am frequently asked whether a retirement income plan should even include Social Security due to the statistics I just mentioned. Fortunately, this issue can be fixed on a napkin. I am literally not kidding. We would eliminate an estimated 50% of the shortfall by increasing the payroll tax 1%. We could also raise the full retirement age for younger works or reduce cost of living adjustments to make a dent. The most effective action would be to eliminate the maximum income in which workers are taxed for Social Security.

These are but a few of the options available to fix the Social Security solvency situation. Since it can be resolved quite simply on paper, I suggest it is more of a political issue that will eventually be resolved, and Social Security should be included in your retirement plan. However, it is wise to run alternative models using reduced benefits in case our politicians do not see this as an issue of importance the same way I do.

In 2020, any employee making over $137,700 does not pay Social Security tax on any dollars earned over that figure. This would basically solve the equation. While this sounds simple, there are pros and cons to each, and the politics of it come into play. Regardless, my point is that I believe that for current and soon-to-be retirees, we should include Social Security as an income stream, but potentially use conservative COLA adjustments when planning on future payments. This is another area where your financial advisor will be able to help by calculating the various probabilities of not outliving your money based on different filing strategies.

Cost of Living

There are some ways you can control your own cost of living: moving to a lower cost area or downsizing your home, for example. But the cost of living you can't control is known as COLA (cost-of-living adjustment). COLA was added to Social Security benefits in 1975. It is meant to help retirees who are living on a fixed income to maintain their standard of living in the face on inflation. COLA increases are based on the consumer price index, the government's official measurement of inflation. It measures the change in price of some 80,000 goods and services. A COLA is automatically triggered when prices go up. For example, a 1.6% COLA went into effect in January 2020. Prior to 1975, Congress had to vote for each change in Social Security benefits.

None of us likes things we can't control, but in reality, **the things beyond your control are less impactful than the things you can control.** Zero percent of your attention should be spent on the things you cannot control, and they should make up the same percentage of your stressors. If you are properly in control of what you can control, you'll do great.

As advisors, we spend a lot of time modeling the things beyond our control to better focus our attention on the controllable actions. For example, when we discussed the Total Return strategy there was a huge difference in successful outcomes at higher cost living increases depending on stock ownership, so during a higher expected period of inflation (cannot control), we may want to hold a higher percentage of stocks (can control).

Chapter 9

Mitigating Risk

A lot of the fears people have about retirement could be alleviated with proper insurance planning. Making sure you have the right kinds of insurance, and enough of it, is critical to retirement planning. Now that you have a retirement budget and know which fruit represents your situation, we can better plan for what I like to call the what-if scenarios.

Protecting your spouse is one of the most important reasons to work with a financial advisor as you plan for retirement. They can help you understand and decide which survivor benefits are appropriate in your situation. That's why you should create a separate budget for the surviving spouse (and why I included it in the prior section). A life insurance policy is not a "gift," something you bestow upon your spouse. In some cases, it is the product that will ensure that your spouse doesn't suffer a significant drop in the quality of life they had when you were alive.

Insurance is one of those things that I think most people underestimate. In all reality, insurance is for things that don't happen very often, but if they do, they can be financially devastating. It's one place, I think, where we've gone wrong with regards to our healthcare, but that's a book for another day.

When you are starting your life out, you might not think about why life insurance would be important. Purchasing permanent life insurance earlier in life can be beneficial because it provides flexibility for later in life. Yet, most individuals in their 20s or 30s don't tend to think about buying life insurance to lock in lower premiums while they're young.

So, the topic of insurance doesn't tend to come up until a significant life event happens, such as marriage and then kids. Life insurance gives you the ability to provide financially for them if you are no longer around, which is why it has been called a gift from the grave.

Disability insurance comes up when you start working, but most employers provide some sort of coverage for disability that covers 60% of your earnings. If your employer gave you a 40% reduction in your paycheck, would you still be able to live in the same manner? Most people might not have enough in emergency savings to cover the difference or would have difficulty changing their lifestyles to adjust for the loss of income. It is something that needs to be considered.

When you do get to retirement, it is important to rethink your insurance plan all over again and revisit what it is that you want to provide should you pass away. There are many things to consider with regard to insurance, especially if you are married and are going to provide for your spouse now that you both have stopped working.

Is there a survivor benefit associated with your pension? How much is it?

Have you adopted the best strategies for maximizing the highest Social Security benefits available to the surviving spouse in the event of the death of the higher earning spouse? Did you know that life insurance can be a very effective estate planning tool to give money, income tax-free, to your kids, grandkids, or church or charity? Some states have an inheritance tax and/or a death tax, and within certain states, some exempt life insurance from this kind of tax.

Mitigating the Risks to Your Plan

"I think of myself as an intelligent, sensitive human being with the soul of a clown which always forces me to blow it at the most important moments."

– Jim Morrison

There are basically three categories of risk that investors face: emotional, behavioral, and financial. I think it's important to cover each briefly.

Emotional

As humans, we make a lot of mistakes because we misperceive reality. Nobel Prize winner Daniel Kahneman's book *Thinking, Fast and Slow* conveys the findings of his lifelong look into what motivates people to make the decisions they do. Basically, it goes like this: We humans tend to think we know more than we actually do, which can get us in trouble as investors. We tend to think what has happened in the most recent past will occur in the future. It is why investors loaded up on tech stocks in the late 1990s, and why in 2005 and 2006 your neighbor was buying rental properties, painting them, and selling them for $75,000 more.

Because prices were going up, investors wanted to jump aboard and thought they could buy a stock or a rental property and make easy money, not necessarily understanding the reality of what was occurring beneath the scenes.

In times of happiness, such as a long bull market, we become irrationally exuberant, as noted by Alan Greenspan years ago. But, when we take in the news, we focus more on the bad stuff than the stories that would enlighten us. I once read that there are 19 negative news stories for every positive one. If our negativity bias already gives more credence to the cruelty of the world, then our unfiltered minds, if left alone, don't stand a chance. Our subconscious minds remember all this information and store it to be acted on later.

This is extremely important to acknowledge because many poor decisions are made based on emotion alone. Thus, if you make fear-based investment decisions, you will miss out on opportunities and the ability to create wealth and security for your family. As I am writing this book, the U.S. stock market took a nasty drop due to the economic threats of the COVID-19 crisis, only to recover rapidly. While the full effects of this crisis are yet to be determined, selling out at that time would have been disastrous for a potential retiree.

Even the steadiest investors can get anxious at times. It is my job as an advisor to reassure clients to stick with the plan, because even the best-laid plan will not work if it is not followed. The investment portfolio follows the plan, and if the plan needs to change, then most likely so does the investment portfolio. Regardless, getting out at the bottom of a temporary decline in U.S. equity prices is a sure-fire way to realize losses that may not recover.

If I saw that your current home was suddenly worth 30% less and told you to sell immediately, you would look at me like I was crazy (because you view your home with a long-term perspective). On the other end of the spectrum, if I told you Amazon was selling everything at 30% off of normal retail prices, you would be online buying up stuff with the excitement my 6-year-old has when she hears the ice cream truck drive by.

I recall one conversation with a retired client couple because the wife used to check her 401k daily while she was still employed. She was an aggressive investor but would become very anxious during recessions and market drops. Her husband was the epitome of stability, joining my words to stay the course during these periods.

Oddly, however, upon retirement they switched roles and *he* began looking at the account balances every day and could not handle seeing any further losses during the pandemic. He wanted to move all their monies to cash and sell out at a substantial loss. Fortunately, his wife and I talked him out of his tree—just in time to benefit from the biggest U.S. stock market gain in history the very next day.

You never know how you are going to react to a fire until your house is burning, but you will definitely call the fire department for help.

Behavioral

When I give talks to our younger generation, I always ask the audience what they think is the biggest reason for financial success. Any guesses? It is very simple. It's your behavior. Your success financially will be driven by how you handle your emotions, understand your biases, and how you act toward your finances. At this point in your life, I'm sure you can think back at your failures and your successes. What do you think was the root cause of each?

For your failures, were you given just bad advice, or did you neglect to follow some sage guidance that your parents, family, friends, mentor, counselor, or advisor offered you? When you failed, did you act first and think later? We all fail at something in life, and the benefit of it is to learn. I do not know a single person involved in sports that has never lost a game.

Participating in sports teaches us the process of preparing to win, but also accepting and learning from loss.

The difference between sports and your retirement is that you get one shot are your retirement. This is game 7 – losing is not an option, so prepare accordingly. Now think about the times that you succeeded at something over the years. Did you do it alone or did you happen to do it with a team, or use the support of someone or something else? Even individual sports, such as wrestling and track and field, have coaches that push athletes to perform better.

My guess is that if you look back at the times you were successful in attaining a certain goal or outcome, it included some form of planning, dedication and diligence, as well as a little patience. It required more faith than fear and there was most likely some sort of assistance and support provided along the way.

It has been said that you can never make the same mistake twice because the second time you make it it's not a mistake, it's a choice.

Financial

Once of the benefits of working with a professional is that it is their duty to analyze and poke holes in the best laid retirement plans so that you are well prepared for a financial shock caused by some unexpected event. Market risk is the potential for your portfolio to drop due to negative economic events. It is said that all boats rise and fall with the tide, but not all as the same time or in the same way. It is why a retirement income plan and portfolio diversification are prudent. However, that is not the only consideration when constructing a portfolio. Through the lens of portfolio risk management, the below risks are viewed as uncertainties and strategies should be created to offset these potential areas.

- **Liquidity** – Not having enough cash or capital to meet expenses
- **Credit** – Investing in companies that may not continue to be profitable
- **Concentration** – Holding too much of your portfolio in one stock
- **Reinvestment** – The inability to reinvest dividends in the same or higher rates as the original holding
- **Interest rate** – The effect of a major change in interest rates will have on your portfolio
- **Inflation** – The need for higher income every year to offset rising costs to live
- **Longevity** – Living much longer than your plan assumed, resulting in a much higher probability of out-living your money.

In addition to these risks, it is very important to understand whether there is a financial risk to your plan if premature death or disability occur. Having the right kind and adequate amounts of insurance can ease a lot of the anxieties people have around retirement. An insurance checkup before retirement can show you any gaps in your plan. Planning ahead may also enable you to pay less and be approved for certain kinds of insurance that get more expensive and harder to qualify for the older you get.

Let's review the various type of insurances and how they may relate to your retirement plan.

Life insurance and your survivor plan
Insurance is meant to reduce the negative impact of things that do not happen very often, but when they do, they can be

financially devastating. If you have a family, you've probably had life insurance for many years. Life insurance is meant to protect your family by allowing those left behind the ability to continue to live with dignity and a reasonable standard of living.

There are two types of life insurance: temporary and permanent. Temporary lasts for a certain period of time and then ends, while permanent lasts forever. In other words, you either are betting on dying soon or living a long life. Obviously, we would all like to bet on a long life but doing so means the life insurance carrier will charge you a greater premium, so we must create an insurance plan that fits your budget.

It is common to purchase temporary life insurance to cover your temporary Needs, to accommodate paying off the mortgage or other debt, to replace income during your working years or your kids' college expenses. Permanent life coverage, on the other hand, would be implemented to provide protection for your entire life, regardless of the situation.

This book is not meant to be a deep dive into which coverage is better (I recommend both to clients depending on their situation and need), but to suggest that when you are entering retirement, you must revisit this to ensure your life insurance plan fits your goals. For example, if your spouse becomes a Pear due to your passing away, the benefit of having life insurance is different than if the survivor would be a Strawberry.

One of the ways life insurance provides protection is to provide a tax-free death benefit that can be used to replace your paycheck if you were to die. But now you're nearing retirement, so you may think you do not need any life coverage, since there is no employment income to replace. You may be thinking that if you have enough investments to retire, then your spouse should be fine. Well, before you automatically make that assumption, let's review your particular situation first.

Will you still be earning income?

If you're planning to retire, you are no longer counting on an income to pay your basic expenses because you have enough guaranteed income in place to do that. After your death, your spouse will continue to receive money from your retirement accounts and Social Security (via the survivor's benefit, but the amount will be less than you received when you were alive). However, maybe there would be a desire to go back to work part time for social purposes.

Do you have debt?

Ideally, you will go into retirement debt free. If you're not there, make a plan to start paying off your remaining debt as soon as possible, particularly if you have high-interest debt like credit card debt.

I stress to my clients how important it is to be debt-free before retirement (it is especially important to be free of federal student loan debt because if you become delinquent, your Social Security can be garnished), but that isn't always possible. Over the past 30 years, the number of homeowners in their 60s and 70s has increased by 50%. And the number of 80-year-olds with a mortgage has increased from 3% to 25%.[22] Forbes's analysis of Federal Reserve data revealed that student loan debt in the same age group has increased 71.5% between 2014 and 2019.[23]

If you are heading into retirement with debt, it means you may not have saved as much for retirement as you will need. Maintaining your life insurance coverage in the face of debt can help protect your spouse.

Are you an empty nester?

If your children are out of the house and self-sufficient, and you and your spouse have sufficient guaranteed income and retirement savings, you may choose to look at options to restructure your life insurance plan. If, however, you have adult children with special needs or your spouse's guaranteed income (in the form of survivor's benefits) would be drastically reduced upon your death, you may want to continue coverage.

Would life insurance help your estate?

Life insurance proceeds can be used strategically for those who have considerable assets. It can be used to pay estate taxes, pay off outstanding business debts, or to fund buy-sell agreements related to your estate or business.

How much life insurance coverage should I have?

What is truly wonderful about The Fruitful Retirement process and strategy is that if you are a survivor, you can follow the same steps noted above to determine your fruit and how to allocate your resources to create a sustainable income stream. Even better, though, is to prepare a retirement budget for both of you together and one for each of you individually.

It is common for a couple to be an Apple or Strawberry with assets and income combined, but should the spouse with a pension predecease the other, the survivor could turn into a Pear—meaning, there now becomes a void in guaranteed income to cover the Needs. If there are not enough assets to provide the guaranteed protection, then additional life insurance may be warranted.

The difference between the retirement budget and the survivor budget is that if there is a shortfall in the retirement budget, it cannot immediately be resolved with taking a red pen to certain variables, such as retirement age or monthly Wants.

If the survivor plan has a shortfall, it can be resolved effectively with the purchase of a life insurance policy.

Long-term care insurance

According to Kiplinger, there is a 70% chance among couples that one of the partners will need some form of long-term care during their lifetime.[24] In fact, according to a survey by Lincoln National Life, 91% of Americans surveyed believe long-term care planning is an important part of retirement planning, yet only 50% of spouses surveyed have discussed it, with many fewer people discussing it with parents or children.[25]

Other than spending too much and the rising cost of living, the biggest risk most retirees face is some sort of personal healthcare crisis.

That could be a function of not being able to perform activities of daily living (bathing, eating, dressing, toileting, continence, transfer) or a cognitive impairment, such as dementia or Alzheimer's (a type of dementia).

Long-term care insurance covers services and support in various settings, including your home and medical facilities.

There are various types of policies to mitigate this risk.

The traditional policy is a standalone approach that reimburses the policyholder a daily amount or monthly dollar figure (up to a preselected limit) for services used, while other traditional policies provide an indemnity benefit that pays the maximum benefit once eligibility occurs. This approach should be viewed similar to a homeowner's or automobile policy in that you hope you never use it but pay pennies to protect the dollars needed down the road should a fire burn down your house, an accident ruin your car, or your mental capacity become diminished. However, these policies have experienced very high premium increases over the last decade and the cost is outpacing the contingent benefits.

For those of you that only desire to pay for it if you use it, and have greater certainty in the premiums you will pay, the hybrid approach may be a better fit. These policies provide both a death and long-term care benefit, essentially giving you back your premiums upon your death if the long-term care benefit is not needed or fully utilized. These have been very popular in recent years. It should be noted that these policies will be more expensive than the traditional approach because they insure you for both mortality and morbidity. Even so, many clients I know have preferred this approach in recent years due to its flexibility and guarantees.

There are also annuity products that offer a long-term care rider that provide additional guaranteed income should extended healthcare become necessary.

A separate strategy that many retirees consider is moving into a continuing care or life community. These communities allow you to simplify your life by transferring all the responsibilities of home ownership to the community, similar to a townhome community. Normally, there is an upfront lump-sum payment to the community, followed by a monthly maintenance fee. There are pros and cons with this option, as you may like where you live and your independence.

I've had clients make the decision to sell their existing home and move into an independent cottage in a continuing care community because it had an active social component to it. They liked the idea that if either one of them went down the course of mental or physical incompetence, the community had the necessary resources to provide the care, while the healthy spouse would not have to worry about moving or being close to the care being provided.

As you can see, there is a range of options and benefits.

The cost of long-term care insurance varies widely, but these are the factors that determine cost:

- Your age at the time you buy the policy
- The maximum amount a policy will pay out per day
- The maximum number of days a policy will pay
- Any optional benefits you choose, like benefits that increase with inflation

If you are already in poor health or receiving long-term care services, you may not qualify for long-term care insurance because most policies require medical underwriting. In that case, you may be able to buy a limited amount of coverage or coverage at a higher rate.

Genworth conducts an annual Cost of Care Survey that not only has a lot of great information but a calculator[26] that lets you see an estimate for the cost of various types of long-term care, in-home, community and assisted living, and nursing home facility according to location. And the calculator has a slider that you can move to see a forecast for costs years into the future.

Below are the median monthly costs in 2019, but please note the cost of long-term care is very specific based on a person's needs and location both in terms of where the caregiving would take place and the area of the country you live in.

In-Home Care
- Homemaker Services: $4,290
- Home-Health Aid: $4,385

Community and Assisted Living
- Adult Day Health Care: $1,625
- Assisted Living Facility: $4,051

Nursing Home Facility
- Semi-Private Room: $7,513
- Private Room: $8,517

Let's take a look at some more of Genworth's findings.[27]

- From 2004 to 2019, the cost for facility and in-home care services has risen on average from 1.71% – 3.64% per year. That's an increase of $892 annually for home care and up to $2,468 annually for a private room in a nursing home. At this rate, some care costs are outpacing the US inflation rate of 2.1% by almost double.
- The world's population is aging at a faster rate than ever before and people are living longer. Every day until 2030, 10,000 Baby Boomers will turn 65 and 7 out of 10 people will require long-term care in their lifetime.
- According to the U.S. Department of Health and Human Services, one in five of today's 65-year-olds who require long-term care or assisted living will need those services for more than five years.[28]

Based on this information, a 65-year-old who spends five years in an assisted living facility will spend $243,000—nearly a quarter of a million dollars.

The AALTCI (American Association for Long-Term Care Insurance) suggests buying long-term insurance between the ages of 52 and 64, but the rate of rejected applications increases with age, so it might be wise to start shopping even earlier.

It should be crystal clear that everyone should have a plan for how to pay for a long-term healthcare scenario. A plan may or may not include insurance to cover this risk, but I'm a firm believer in planning up front, so you do not have to manage crises down the road. It is unfair to put the burden of caring for you solely on your spouse, family, or friends should you reach the point of needing more care that non-professionals are equipped to handle.

It should also be very clear that it is in your best interest to have assistance in truly understanding what options are available and which are the best fit for you. This is merely another reason that engaging the services of a financial planner is to your benefit.

I had a situation with a client who had been a widow for ten years and all her children lived across country. Her mind was sharp, but her physical ailments resulted in her needing care at home full time. She had a policy that she had purchased a long time ago at the suggestion of her husband when he was alive, but the agent had since retired and she was having great difficulty claiming her rightful benefits. While we were able to help her in the end, the time, frustration, and financial costs could have been avoided.

Medical insurance & prescriptions

The outrageous cost of medical care in the United States is no secret, but the numbers and consequences may be worse than you realized.

By the time you reach 65 years old, average healthcare costs are $11.3K per person, per year in the United States. This is nearly triple the annual average cost of when you're in your 20s and 30s. During one's lifetime, over $400K will be spent on the average American's healthcare in today's dollars. And that is if medical costs rise at the same rate as inflation. If medical costs rise at 3% more than inflation, your healthcare will cost over $2MM, the vast majority of which will take place after the age of 45.

Even if your insurance company or Medicare covers most of that bill, the typical American can still be on the hook for a very large sum of money to cover their health-care costs as they age.

The rate of senior citizens declaring bankruptcy has more than doubled since 1999, and the leading cause is high healthcare costs. Despite the existence of Medicare insurance for seniors, it doesn't cover all costs and healthcare can be extremely expensive, especially as you age.[29]

Most people aged 65 and older will be eligible for Medicare. If you reach that age and are still working and your employer-sponsored coverage is better than Medicare, you can keep it; but Medicare imposes a late enrollment penalty for people who don't sign up for Medicare Part B (coverage for medical treatment and supplies) and Part D (coverage for prescription drugs) when they become age-eligible. That penalty may not apply if you have group medical coverage through your employer but be sure to confirm that before declining enrollment at 65.

Because Medicare doesn't cover 100% of medical expenses, you should consider buying supplemental coverage like Medigap or a Medicare Advantage Plan offered by a private insurance company to fill in coverage gaps. There are professionals that specialize in helping to provide guidance on which plan is the best fit for you. For my clients that are over 65 and need supplemental coverage, I put them in touch with one of these specialists.

Another potential cost is the prescription drugs that you may need. I highly recommend writing down a full list of your medications that you are taking and make sure your doctors have that list. Next time you are at the doctor, show him or her the list and ask if there are any cheaper alternatives. If there are not, you can still compare prices for certain prescriptions on sites such as WellRx.com and GoodRx.com.

Another side benefit to providing that list to your doctor is that these drugs have side effects, and your doctor knowing everything you are taking may help with suggesting an alternative drug. Creating this list at home will save your sanity when attempting to remember it at the doctor's office. I would be hard pressed to recall what I ate this morning, much less remember the names and doses of my five daily supplements.

Homeowner's or renter's insurance Mortgage lenders require homeowners to have insurance, but once your mortgage is paid, there is nothing stopping you from canceling your policy. Apart from common sense, of course. I know none of you reading this would cancel your homeowner's insurance. I just want to make you aware of a few things you might not think of when it comes to protecting your possessions with insurance.

If you choose to move to a new area of the country when you retire, you may need to buy additional insurance that will cover damage caused by a natural disaster that regular homeowner's insurance doesn't cover. If you downsize into an apartment, you will need renter's insurance. People sometimes mistakenly believe that whatever insurance the building owner pays for covers their property in the event of damage, but that isn't the case. If your property is damaged or stolen, or someone is injured in your apartment, you will be responsible. Fortunately, renter's insurance is very inexpensive, so there is no reason not to buy it.

Travel insurance

If extensive or prolonged international travel is part of your retirement plans, it might be advisable to buy comprehensive travel insurance. Look for a policy that covers the trip itself, (delays and cancellations) and medical care, including medical evacuation. But before you start policy shopping, read the fine print for your credit cards, particularly travel rewards cards. These cards often cover a lot of the same things comprehensive travel insurance covers and at no extra cost, simply as a perk of the card.

Chapter 10

Planning for Retirement

What consumes your mind is what controls your life.

– Anonymous

Planning for retirement is a multi-step process.

Retirement Income Planning Process

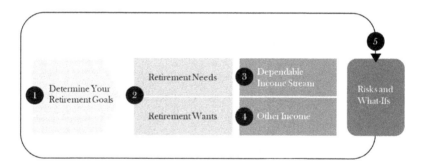

Assemble a Team

If you've been DIYing your finances up to this point, it's time to consider getting some professional help. When you were younger, the stakes were lower. If you made some poor financial decisions, you had plenty of time to learn and recover from those mistakes.

But the same can't be said for retirement. Any mistakes you make now could have devastating consequences for you, your family, and your Legacy. The margin for error is small, so now is the time to assemble a team of professionals who can guide you through retirement.

At the end of the book, I provide a list of credentials that you may see from financial advisors along with what they mean and the requirements to attain and maintain them.

CFP

Engaging an advisor that holds a CFP® designation can help you create a plan and also tweak a portfolio based on your retirement time horizon and risk tolerance. He or she can provide you with strategies to help you work toward living the kind of Fruitful Retirement you've been dreaming of. And perhaps most importantly, a CFP can help bring clarity about your retirement.

Estate Planning Attorney

There are a lot of moving parts to an estate plan—a will, financial power of attorney, medical power of attorney, advanced medical directive, and a revocable living trust, to name a few. You can create some or all of these documents with online DIY sites, but doing so could lead to all kinds of problems if you fail to cross every *t* and dot every *i*, including invalidation of those documents.

An estate planning attorney can do a lot more than just draw up the necessary papers. He or she can guide you on issues like choosing the right person for your powers of attorney and deciding if setting up a trust is appropriate for your situation. Your CFP® will work with your attorney in the background to ensure both your investments are in sync with your estate plan.

Tax Preparer/CPA

A CPA can save you time by ensuring you are filing your taxes properly and not overpaying Uncle Sam. I say often that I'm proud to be an American and pay my taxes, but I'm just as happy to pay half the tax if it is legal. A CPA can also work with your CFP® to discuss any tax planning techniques that will be beneficial for you, up to and into retirement.

Insurance Agent

An Insurance agent can save you time by helping to protect the various risks that you come across in life, such as dying prematurely, becoming disabled, needing long-term healthcare, getting into a car accident, a house fire, or getting sued. In many cases, your CFP® will create a comprehensive plan to address these risks. Sometimes that professional can analyze the various policies in the marketplace and provide you a solution. Other times, any insurance products that need to be purchased are outsourced to another professional that specializes in that particular type of coverage. Whether your CFP® offers insurance products is irrelevant, but they should have a plan created for you to address the what-if scenarios listed above to ensure you are protected if any of those circumstances occur.

Retirement Goals

This is not just the date that you would like to discontinue employment, but also begin the activities you would like to do once that period begins. I like to tell my clients that if you can tell me how you are going to spend your time in retirement, I can better help you spend your money. It is silly to go to the grocery store without a list of the items you plan to purchase. If you are like me, you end up leaving with a few extra items because something looked delicious. (Side note: do NOT go to the grocery store hungry.)

Retirement Income Planning Expenses

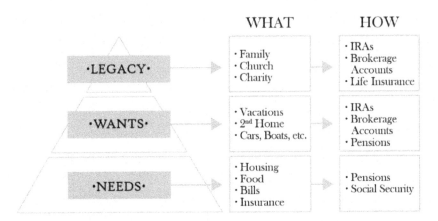

Well, it is also silly to not enter retirement without an idea of what you will be doing with your time. Now that you have gone through the earlier exercises, you may have some ideas of your added activities in retirement. Some will cost money. Others will not. Just like my trips to the grocery store, there will inevitably be items or activities that were not initially included on your list, but having an idea of your goals is a great place to start planning.

Visualizing your ideal retirement is really the focus of this book. But in this section, we are largely focusing on the money side of retirement planning so think about whether you want to continue to work in some capacity during retirement and if so, for how long. Don't keep working to maximize short term return. Keep working to minimize long term regret.

Whether or not you are still going to have money coming in from a paycheck will impact your retirement planning decisions.

Decide Where to Live

You may have been tied to an area of the country with a high cost of living or that you didn't like. Once you quit working, you are free to live wherever you choose. If you are a Pear, moving to a place with a low cost of living may be a necessary decision. If you're a Strawberry, moving to a state with a more favorable tax situation may be one of the strategies you use to preserve your Legacy.

Another decision is what type of housing you're going to live in. Many empty nesters choose to downsize both in terms of size and maintenance, which means they move into an apartment or condo.

I cannot tell you how many clients I have counseled over the years that made the decision to move but, if a couple, one of them was very hesitant to do so. The planning process allows for clarity and the reduction of fear-based decisions. Moving is a big decision, especially near or at retirement. I have found over the years that having an independent, non-emotional financial planner telling a couple "You can do it" really does push that process along in a way that changes the ballgame from a 9th-inning nail-biter filled with anxiety and fear to one focused on the excitement of the experience and the love of the game.

Review your Pension Plans

The payout for your pension depends on how long you were with the company and your salary. When you retire, you can choose between a lump-sum payment or a monthly annuity payment. Pensions aren't portable the way a 401k is. You can't take it with you to a new employer or roll it over into an IRA. When you retire, you must contact the people who run the pension fund at your previous company and apply for your benefit.

You cannot access your pension until retirement age, which is typically 65, but some plans allow you to start collecting early retirement benefits as early as age 55. If you choose to receive benefits early, the monthly payment will be less than if you wait until retirement age.

Unlike other retirement accounts, you cannot take a loan from your pension.

Taking your pension as a monthly annuity can help provide steady income, something especially important for Pears. If you choose to take a lump sum, you are able to choose how to invest it. If you do not have a lot of experience investing your own money, a professional can show you your options and help you choose the best one for you.

If you have some doubt about the future of the company, a lump-sum distribution may be the better option, even for Pears who could use the money to buy another form of annuity. If you choose monthly payments and the company goes under, you could lose out. Even if your company is protected under the Pension Benefits Guarantee Corporation, the PBGC does not guarantee that it will cover 100% of the money you were supposed to be paid.

If you choose the monthly annuity, you will have another choice to make. A single-life annuity lasts the lifetime of the pension holder. A joint-and-survivor annuity will continue to pay your spouse after your death.

Of course, the single-life annuity monthly payment is larger than the joint-and-survivor annuity because the expected payment period is shorter. It is important to make the right choice because in most cases, you can't change your mind down the road.

Chapter 11
Taxes and Estate Planning

*Death, taxes and childbirth! There's never
any convenient time for any of them.*

– Margaret Mitchell, *Gone with the Wind*

In a 1789 Letter Benjamin Franklin wrote, "Our new constitution has been established and has an appearance that promises permanency, but nothing can be certain except death and taxes." Well, when it comes to retirement, nothing that Ben Franklin said has changed.

The only thing we can say is certain are his two words. In fact, taxes may end up taking far more of your retirement dollars then the stock market, so it is important to plan for the income-tax effect, as well as any death and/or inheritance taxes.

When we retire, we basically have assets that fall into three different categories when it comes to your taxes. They either are fully taxable at your ordinary income tax rates, they're partially taxable at capital gains rates, or they're tax free. Depending on the type of investment or position you hold will determine how it is taxed.

This becomes very important when looking at creating a sustainable income stream for retirement because of the way that the U.S. tax system works. It's a progressive system, meaning the more you make, the more they take. And once you go above a certain amount, you move into what we call the marginal tax rate, where you pay more taxes. It makes sense, then, to plan appropriately so that you stay within a certain tax bracket.

To do this requires planning prior to retirement as well as making adjustments as you distribute money during retirement.

As we discussed in the planning and budgeting section, the first thing to do is to get an idea of your Needs, your Wants, and your Legacy desires. Once you've done that and compared against the income sources and asset availability that you have, we can come up with a plan.

It would be unwise and imprudent to not include the tax effect in all of this. The other thing to think about when it comes to Legacy is how you will be taxed on the monies that you leave behind. The federal government has an exemption as of the writing of this book of over $11.4M per person. Meaning, a married couple needs an estate valued at over $22.8M to pay a federal death tax. However, as tax and estate laws change, I would be surprised if these figures did not change with them in the future.

On top of all of that, states get their piece of your pie as well. In fact, 18 states charge an estate or inheritance tax upon death. Below I've listed each state that charges estate taxes[30] and the amount of the state's exemption to help you determine whether your heirs will face an estate tax liability in the year 2020.

Death Tax States

- Connecticut – $5,100,000
- District of Columbia – $5,600,000
- Hawaii – $5,490,000
- Illinois – $4,000,000
- Oregon – $1,0500,000
- Maine – $5,700,000

- Maryland – $5,000,000
- Massachusetts – $1,000,000
- Minnesota – $3,000,000
- New York – $5,850,000
- Rhode Island – $1,579,922
- Vermont – $4,250,000
- Washington – $2,193,000

Inheritance Tax States

- Iowa – 0% - 16%
- Kentucky – 0% - 16%
- Maryland – 10%
- Nebraska – 1% - 18%
- New Jersey – 11% - 16%
- Pennsylvania – 4.5% - 15%

Many people believe that if you have a will you don't need an estate plan, that you have to have a huge amount of wealth before you need an estate plan, or that you should be close to retirement age before creating an estate plan. All of these are misconceptions. **If you have dependents or assets, you should create an estate plan.**

An estate plan means you and your family, not the state where you reside, will make decisions about where your assets go. And having an estate plan isn't only about money. If you were in some way mentally or physically unable to make decisions for yourself, and only your name was on the title of your assets, a court-appointed representative would determine how those assets should be disbursed for your care.

In just about any circumstance you can imagine, becoming incapacitated or dying without an estate plan can be a nightmare for you and your family. When you die without an estate, your state's probate laws will determine how your assets are to be distributed. If you have minor children and both you and the other parent die, the court will decide who gets guardianship of your children.

Wills and trusts are two of the most popular estate planning tools. Wills and trusts are not mutually exclusive. Both allow you to spell out how you would like your property to be distributed, but they go far beyond that.

Just about everyone needs a will. Besides enabling you to determine the distribution of your property, a will gives you the opportunity to nominate your executor and guardians for your minor children. Bear in mind that property distributed through your will is subject to probate, which can be a time-consuming and costly process.

Trusts differ from wills in that trusts are actual legal entities. Like a will, trusts spell out how you want your property distributed. Trusts let you customize the distribution of your estate with the added advantages of property management and probate avoidance. While trusts offer numerous advantages, they incur upfront costs and ongoing administrative fees. The use of trusts also involves a complex web of tax rules and regulations. You should consider the counsel of an experienced estate planning professional and your legal and tax advisers before implementing such a strategy.

Incapacity poses almost as much of a threat to your financial well-being as death does. Fortunately, there are tools that can help you cope with this threat.

A durable power of attorney is a legal agreement that avoids the need for a conservatorship and enables you to designate who will make your legal and financial decisions if you become incapacitated. Unlike the standard power of attorney, durable powers remain valid if you become incapacitated.

Similar to the durable power of attorney, a health care proxy is a document in which you designate someone to make your health care decisions for you if you are incapacitated. The person you designate can generally make decisions regarding medical facilities, medical treatments, surgery, and a variety of other health care issues. Much like the durable power of attorney, the health care proxy involves some important decisions. Take the utmost care when choosing who will make them.

A related document, the living will—also known as a directive to physicians or a health care directive—spells out the kinds of life-sustaining treatment you will permit in the event of your incapacitation. The directive creates an agreement between you and the attending physician. The decision for or against life support is one that only you can make. That makes the living will a valuable estate planning tool. You may also use a living will in conjunction with a durable health care power of attorney. Bear in mind that laws governing the recognition and treatment of living wills may vary from state to state.

As you can see, an estate is not just an essential part of retirement planning, it is an essential part of life planning.

The Documents for Your Estate Plan

One of the best gifts you can give a loved one is an organized estate. If you have ever had to administer a loved one's estate, you will know what I'm talking about. Don't be silly and think that estate planning is all about you. It's not. **So, don't do it for yourself; do it for the ones you love.**

As you probably imagine, there are many pieces to a complete estate plan.

- **A Will**: While a will is not enough to ensure that you and your family are taken care of exactly as you wish, it is an important part of your estate plan.
- **A Trust**: A trust is a legal entity in which you place your assets and will be managed by a neutral party called a trustee. Once you place assets into a trust, they no longer belong to you; they belong to the trust and will be managed by the trustee.
- **Power of Attorney**: The person to whom you give power of attorney can make medical and financial decisions if you are unable to do so.
- **Living Will**: This document outlines any medical procedures you want or don't want to be used in the case of life-threatening illness or injury at a time when you are incapable of communicating your desires.
- **Digital Estate Plan**: In recent years, most states have adopted the Revised Uniform Fiduciary Access to Digital Assets Act, which allows you to grant access to your digital assets to a legal representative upon death. Consult your attorney to create an inventory of your digital assets and preferences to include in your will. Also, certain online services allow for access to your accounts after you die. For example, Facebook has a memorialization settings page, and Google will let you select trusted contacts who can access your Gmail.

Other Important Documents

All important information and documents pertaining to your finances, legal matters, and estate should be kept in a central file and accessible to your executor. All the careful estate planning in the world won't matter if no one can find the documents they need to carry out your wishes. Be sure to include the following in that central file:

- Letter of last instructions
- Medical records
- Bank and brokerage statements
- Income and gift tax returns
- Insurance policies
- Titles and deeds
- Will and trust documents

In Conclusion – You Own This!

*Take action: Success is not guaranteed
but inaction will guaranty failure.*

– Ken Poirot

Let's recap what you just read. Retirement is complex, and it can be scary to think about. But, at some point, most people go through the stages of acknowledgment, anxiety, action and, finally, acceptance. It is vitally important that anyone in the stage of acknowledging a potential retirement in the next five years (or who has recently retired) redefine what it truly is they want out of the rest of their life. Financial independence means having the time to focus on the activities that bring joy and peace to our lives.

Redefine retirement according to you, from where you will live to how you will spend your time. Give yourself purpose and meaning in this new identity, but don't forget about all the wonderful skills you have acquired so far in the journey. Understand you are not in this alone and an open line of communication with those you love is important during this transition.

Focus on what you can control, such as your spending, your plan, and doing what you can to stay fit, both mentally and physically. Expending energy on things we cannot control is a loss leader and returns nothing but anxiety and wasted effort, but applying that same energy to what you love and brings you peace is the oxygen for a Fruitful Retirement.

Hire a team to give you experience and expertise on your side. If this is the biggest decision of your life, why would you not want a team of professionals that do this for a living as your personal guide on this journey. I am certain you do not make all the decisions at the office without consulting other well-informed professionals, so why do it with your own retirement?

Complete a retirement budget to determine which fruit you are and plan accordingly. Complete a survivor budget and follow the same steps, knowing that the surviving spouse will most likely be a different fruit and need to plan differently.

Pears do not have enough guaranteed retirement income to cover their Needs. Apples have enough guaranteed retirement income to cover their Needs but not their Wants. Strawberries have enough guaranteed retirement income to cover both.

You can move up the ladder from a Pear to an Apple to a Strawberry. Knowing which one you are will allow you to better create the best financial strategy to maximize your wealth and security and mitigate potential risks.

Finally, I thank you for reading my book, as it is a culmination of my adult life spent helping others reach their potential. I wrote it because I have found over the years that if there is one common theme to everyone's retirement it can be summed up in this one word: time. In life, the most precious thing we have is the time to spend doing what we are meant to do. Time is scarce and cannot be retrieved once lost. It is truly the essence of what most people are looking for—the freedom and ability to do what brings them joy.

As Americans, we say we value freedom above all else, but we also know inherently that freedom is not free. Many have come before us and dedicated their lives to preserving the ideals of life, liberty and the pursuit of happiness. It is with much gratitude to those that have spent their journey in an effort to allow us to enjoy an infinite range of opportunities. It makes sense, then, that if we want the freedom to spend our time as we wish, we must commit some of it to ensuring its sustainability.

Final Acceptance

Remember when we discussed acceptance as the final stage of retirement earlier in the book? I was referring to it as the *emotional* acceptance of retirement. It comes when you've arrived at that place *and* when you accept that yes, you have done things right. All of those years of working and planning have paid off. You can trust that you will not outlive your money and that you will have the kind of Fruitful Retirement that you have dreamed of.

You've done it. I hope this book has been helpful to you in finding both acceptance and final acceptance. It was my great pleasure.

I truly hope you live The Fruitful Retirement!

Appendix

Choosing an Advisor

I strongly believe that having professional help can make a tremendous difference when it comes to financial planning in general, and retirement planning in particular. But having the right help matters too. If you are looking for professional financial help, here are some thoughts.

The purpose of this book is not to replace the relationship you have with your financial advisor, but rather to enhance it. If you are not currently working with an advisor, then hopefully you have a good place to start. Either way, when entering retirement, it is important to have a team to support you, and that includes revisiting your current relationships to ensure that they are best suited to help you move forward.

Most important is that you feel that your advisor will put your needs first and keep your best interest in mind when creating a strategy and guiding you through financial decisions. This really comes down to trust.

When you are searching for an advisor, you will notice many have different credentials behind their name. Each represents a different kind of specialty and requires different levels of training and testing, as well as so many hours of continuing education to keep those credentials.

See below for some of the most important credentials in the marketplace today.

CFP® (Certified Financial Planner)

I would consider this the most important credential when hiring a financial advisor. These professionals are well versed in many financial topics. To become a CFP®, a professional must complete courses from a CFP® board-registered program in the areas of financial planning, risk management and insurance planning, retirement savings and income planning, investment planning, education, and estate planning. After that, a 7-hour exam follows, on which they must score 70% to pass. Somewhere in the neighborhood of 30 – 40% fail the first time they take it. Finally, they must complete 6,000 hours of professional experience related to the financial planning process or complete an apprenticeship of 4,000 hours that meets supplemental requirements.

Once they become a CFP®, they must complete 30 hours of continuing education every two years, with a requirement for ethics.

Just as medical doctors have differing approaches and opinions to diagnose and prescribe treatment for their patients, different CFP® professionals may have different thoughts and strategies for their clients on how to best reach their goals and manage money. Physicians are obligated to adhere to the Hippocratic Oath to treat the ill to the best of their ability, preserve their patients' privacy, and share knowledge with those to follow. Similarly, the CFP® board maintains a standard of professional conduct that details our code of ethics and professional responsibility, including integrity, objectivity, competence, fairness, confidentiality, professionalism, and diligence. The board outlines practice standards and the financial planning process by which CFPs agree to live and hold themselves accountable.

In other words, this is an important credential, but only held by around 25% of financial advisors.

CPA *(Certified Public Accountant)*

While this license is geared toward accountants, tax preparers, and financial analysts, I include it here because I would venture to say it is one of the most widely recognized certifications in the industry today. To become a CPA, a professional must have 150 hours of college credits and pass the CPA exam. It is tested in four sections, each four hours long. The sections are auditing and attestation, financial accounting and reporting, regulation, and business environment and concepts.

You may think, at first read, that this does not relate well to personal financial planning, but CPAs have a two-year experience requirement under a CPA and a very difficult exam to pass (around 50% pass rate) to attain this credential. The American Institute for CPAs has a code of conduct based on six principles: responsibilities, serving the public interest, integrity, objectivity and independence, due care, and scope and nature of services.

While most CPAs are either controllers, CFOs, tax preparers, financial analysts, accountants, or auditors, some eventually transition into the financial planning and advisory arena. The benefit of having a CPA as a financial advisor is that most likely they have a diverse background in the business world, are very good with numbers, and understand the tax code well.

The continuing education requirement for CPAs is 80 hours every two years, with certain ethics requirements. That is a full week per year dedicated to updating their education of real-time topics. This is key for any professional, and it should give you some comfort knowing that your adviser is required to keep up with the industry.

ChFC *(Chartered Financial Consultant)*

This certification was created as an alternative to the CFP. The topics studied are very similar to the CFP and, in fact, more coursework is required, but instead of passing a comprehensive board exam following the coursework, the ChFC takes a test at the end of each class.

It should be noted that even though a ChFC has not passed a rigorous comprehensive exam, this professional still has thoroughly studied financial planning, insurance planning, retirement needs, investments, estate planning, employee benefits, tax planning, and asset protection.

Each ChFC professional must complete 30 hours of continuing education every two years, along with ethics requirements, just like the CFP® professional

CFA (Chartered Financial Analyst)

Administered by the CFA Institute, and labeled as the most recognized investment management designation in the world, these professionals have to master 10 investment topics and pass three levels of extremely difficult exams before they can practice.

This credential is wonderful, but you are not likely to find it among professionals providing financial planning guidance. Most financial advisors or firms that you would work with have CFAs on staff or are utilizing the expertise of many CFAs within their network or broker/dealer. If you are solely looking for somebody to invest and manage your money without the financial planning guidance, then you would look for this credential.

CLU (Chartered Life Underwriter)

This certification is the best one for insurance agents. This professional has to take eight courses administered by the American College of Financial Planning. While there is no comprehensive exam like those required for the CFP® or CPA, these professionals are experts in life insurance, estate planning, and risk management.

Questions to ask a potential financial advisor:

Most important, in my opinion, is not the questions that you ask a potential advisor, but the questions that they ask *you.* If the advisor spends your time talking about himself instead of asking questions to get to know you, it should be apparent the focus is not you. That said, here are a few questions to ask the advisor:

1. Are you a fiduciary?
2. What is your financial planning process and retirement income strategy?
3. What qualifications and certifications do you have?
4. Do you have any disciplinary history? If so, for what type of conduct?
5. How do you charge for your services?
6. What is your investment management process?
7. Who actually manages the money?

101 Things to Do in Retirement

1. Plant a garden
2. Write a book
3. Go on walks
4. Practice yoga
5. Relocate seasonally
6. Volunteer with a local nonprofit that gives you a sense of purpose
7. Renovate your home
8. Visit the children (or grandchildren) more often
9. Start a consulting business
10. Meet new friends at Meetup.com
11. Read
12. Write a blog
13. Practice martial arts or Tai Chi
14. Volunteer
15. Go to the theater
16. Make wine
17. Go wine tasting
18. Woodworking
19. Go fishing
20. Grow flowers
21. Dance
22. Study geology
23. Golf
24. Hike
25. Ride horses
26. Join a band

27. Learn an instrument
28. Sign up for a half-marathon
29. Go kayaking or canoeing
30. Fly kites
31. Go on picnics
32. Go snorkeling
33. Snowboard
34. Ski
35. Swim
36. Do Zumba
37. Knit
38. Crochet
39. Do CrossFit
40. Do crossword puzzles
41. Learn to cook or bake
42. Compose music
43. Bike
44. Play board games
45. Participate in a book club
46. Play baseball
47. Play basketball
48. Practice archery
49. Create art
50. Study astronomy
51. Go back to school
52. Become an activist
53. Go antiquing
54. Camp
55. Play chess
56. Collect something interesting
57. Learn to mix drinks (mixology)
58. Go museum hopping

59. Ride a motorcycle
60. Photography
61. Sew
62. Go scuba diving
63. Sailing
64. Rock climbing
65. Roller skating
66. Rowing
67. Make movies
68. Clean the house
69. Crafts
70. Genealogy
71. 3D Printing
72. Join or start a band
73. Brew beer
74. Keep bees
75. Visit the local zoo
76. Visit the local aquarium
77. Become an actor and join a local theater group
78. Try out for the Senior Olympics
79. Sculpt
80. Paint
81. Make pottery
82. Go 4-wheeling
83. Hunt
84. Design clothing
85. Throw darts
86. repair electronics
87. Meditate
88. Practice calligraphy
89. Be a mentor or coach
90. Make and sell jewelry

91. Journal
92. Paragliding
93. Learn a foreign language
94. Fix cars
95. Play poker
96. Become an expert at anything
97. Get in the best shape of your life
98. Reconnect with prior acquaintances and friends
99. Go to adult summer camp
100. Become an ornithologist (study birds)
101. Travel

Quality-of-life Technologies that Can Change Your Life

Moore's Law suggests that we can expect the speed and capability of technology to double about every two years. There are some wonderful, life-changing technologies in the marketplace, and I only see the range of possibilities of life experiences expanding. These quality-of-life applications can help you maintain your independence as you age. Here are a few areas that I see as potentially beneficial to you. Identify a few you like and try them out.

Just as you would analyze a new process, method, or tech application at work, do the same at home.

ONLINE LEARNING

Just because you plan to retire does *not* mean you should cancel your journey to increased knowledge. In fact, you will finally have the time to learn about something you enjoy instead of having to sit through another Webex conference for professional credits or licensing requirements.

- Coursera
- edX
- Khan Academy
- Lynda.com
- Udacity
- One Day University (onedayu.com)
- Masterclass.com

SOCIAL NETWORKS

I discussed this earlier in the book. It is vital that you have a plan for staying socially connected. That means different things to different people, but knowing what it means to you will prove to be the fruit in your retirement.

- Connected Living
- Buzz50
- Meetup.com
- 50Connect
- Our Time (for the singles out there)
- Yahoo Groups (groups.yahoo.com)
- Senior Chatters (Facebook)
- Older Is Wiser

MOBILITY

In a recent survey by AARP (American Association of Retired Persons), 90% of respondents expected to age in their own home. It makes sense, as we are comfortable with continuity and the thought of moving can be challenging. There are contractors called CAPS (Certified Aging- in-Place Specialists) that will help to retrofit your current home to support your aging in place.

AAA spokesman Michael Green stated: "Older Americans who have stopped driving are almost two times more likely to suffer from depression and nearly five times as likely to enter a long-term care facility compared to those who remain behind the wheel."[31] I found this fascinating, and while you may want to continue driving, having the ability to order in more often is not a bad thing. You might consider some of the services below.

- Uber and UberEats
- Amazon Fresh

- Peapod
- Blue Apron
- Brubhub
- Peach Dish

HOUSEKEEPING

Here are a few apps that can help you find information when you need it, or find the people to help you do it.

- Google Chrome or Amazon Echo
- Angie's List
- Home Advisor
- TaskRabbit
- Thumbtack
- Delivery.com

HEALTHCARE

As mentioned above, health care very likely may be the largest expense during retirement, whether it is a proactive or reactive expense. Here are a few apps that can help.

- Fitbit
- AARP rx
- Medisafe
- Carecierge

FORBES TOP 25 PLACES TO RETIRE[32]

1. Athens, GA
2. Bella Vista, AR
3. Boise, ID

4. Brevard, NC
5. Charlotte, NC
6. Clearwater, FL
7. Columbia, MO
8. Delray Beach, FL
9. Fargo, ND
10. Green Valley, AZ
11. Iowa City, IA
12. Jacksonville, FL
13. Lawrence, KS
14. Lexington, KY
15. Maryville, TN
16. Palm Bay, FL
17. Pittsburgh, PA
18. Rochester, MN
19. San Antonio, TX
20. San Marcos, TX
21. Sarasota, FL
22. Savannah, GA
23. Sun City, AZ
24. Wenatchee, WA
25. Winchester, VA

I would be remiss to not mention my hometown of Carlisle, Pennsylvania. It's worth a visit so check it out!

ENDNOTES

1. Stevenson, Betsey. "Subjective Well-Being and Income: Is There Any Evidence of Satiation?" *Brookings*, 28 July 2016, www.brookings.edu/research/subjective-well%E2%80%90being-and-income-is-there-any-evidence-of-satiation.

2. Kahneman, Daniel. "High Income Improves Evaluation of Life but Not Emotional Well-Being." *PNAS*, 21 Sept. 2010, www.pnas.org/content/107/38/16489.

3. Jebb, Andrew. "Happiness, Income Satiation and Turning Points around the World." *Nature Human Behaviour*, 8 Jan. 2018, www.nature.com/articles/s41562-017-0277-0?error=cookies_not_supported&code=5172e2c8-c674-43f0-b1b6-851caa1f0579.

4. "World Happiness Report 2017 | The World Happiness Report." *World Happiness Report*, 20 Mar. 2017, worldhappiness.report/ed/2017.

5. Merrill Lynch. "Health and Retirement: Planning for the Great Unknown." *AgeWave.Com*, 2014, agewave.com/wp-content/uploads/2016/07/2014-ML-AW-Health-and-Retirement_Planning-for-the-Great-Unknown.pdf.

6. "The Importance of Having a Sense of Purpose: Recent Study Links Strong Life Purpose and Health." *Psychology Today*, 4 June 2019, www.psychologytoday.com/us/blog/flourish-and-thrive/201906/the-importance-having-sense-purpose.

7. "The Mental Health Benefits Of Having A Daily Routine." *The Blurt Foundation*, 8 Nov. 2018, www.blurtitout.org/2018/11/08/mental-health-benefits-routine.

8. "The Health Benefits of Socializing: Four Reasons to Connect with Friends." *Psychology Today*, 30 June 2016, www.psychologytoday.com/us/blog/living-mild-cognitive-impairment/201606/the-health-benefits-socializing.

9. https://www.nytimes.com/#publisher. "Social Ties Reduce Risk of a Cold." *Https://Www.Nytimes.Com/#publisher*, 25 June 1997, www.nytimes.com/1997/06/25/us/social-ties-reduce-risk-of-a-cold.html.

10. "You Are Not Your Work: How to Escape 'Workism' and Reclaim Your Identity." *Psychology Today*, 26 Mar. 2019, www.psychologytoday.com/us/blog/tracking-wonder/201903/you-are-not-your-work.

11. "Spirituality." *Psychology Today*, www.psychologytoday.com/us/basics/spirituality.

12. Alimujiang, Aliya Mph. "Association Between Life Purpose and Mortality Among US Adults Older Than 50 Years." *Cardiology | JAMA Network Open | JAMA Network*, 24 May 2019, jamanetwork.com/journals/jamanetworkopen/fullarticle/2734064.

13. Powell, Colin. "Kids Need Structure." *TED Talks*, www.ted.com/talks/colin_powell_kids_need_structure/transcript?language=en. Accessed 12 July 2020.

14. Robinson, Lawrence. "Volunteering and Its Surprising Benefits - HelpGuide. Org." *Help Guide*, www.helpguide.org/articles/healthy-living/volunteering-and-its-surprising-benefits.htm. Accessed 12 July 2020.

15. "Zac Brown Band - Chicken Fried Lyrics | AZLyrics.Com." *AZ Lyrics*, www. azlyrics.com/lyrics/zacbrownband/chickenfried.html. Accessed 12 July 2020.

16. "A History of the S&P 500 Dividend Yield." *Investopedia*, www.investopedia. com/articles/markets/071616/history-sp-500-dividend-yield.asp#:%7E:text= Between%20January%20and%20June%202016,during%20the%20previous %20five%20years. Accessed 12 July 2020.

17. Hartsook, Tyler. "Will Your Spending Go Down in Retirement?" *Gratus Capital*, 4 Jan. 2019, gratuscapital.com/2019/01/02/will-your-spending-go-down-in-retirement.

18. Leonhardt, Megan. "Americans Now Spend Twice as Much on Health Care as They Did in the 1980s." *CNBC*, 9 Oct. 2019, www.cnbc.com/2019/10/09/ americans-spend-twice-as-much-on-health-care-today-as-in-the-1980s.html.

19. "Genetics Loads the Gun, Environment Pulls the Trigger." *MedCraveOnline. Com*, Journal of Nutritional Health and Food Engineering, medcraveonline. com/JNHFE/JNHFE-03-00107.pdf. Accessed 12 July 2020.

20. "Retirement & Survivors Benefits: Life Expectancy Calculator." *Social Security*, www.ssa.gov/OACT/population/longevity.html. Accessed 12 July 2020.

21. "Trustees Report Summary." *Social Security*, 22 Apr. 2020, www.ssa.gov/oact/ TRSUM/index.html.

22. Studies, Joint Center For Housing. "Housing America's Older Adults 2019 | Joint Center for Housing Studies of Harvard University." *Joint Center for Housing Studies*, www.jchs.harvard.edu/housing-americas-older-adults-2019. Accessed 12 July 2020.

23. Farrington, Robert. "The Growing Trend Of Retiree Student Loan Debt." *Forbes*, 22 May 2019, www.forbes.com/sites/robertfarrington/2019/05/22/the-growing-trend-of-retiree-student-loan-debt/#412ddafe46a4.

24. Lankford, Kimberly. "How to Afford Long-Term Care." *Kiplinger*, 31 Jan. 2019, www.kiplinger.com/article/insurance/t036-c000-s002-how-to-afford-long-term-care.html.

25. "4 Myths Fact Sheet." *Lincoln Financial Group*, lincolnfinancial.lookbookhq. com/mgt3-icc/mgr-conv-fli007. Accessed 12 July 2020.

26. "Cost of Long Term Care by State | Cost of Care Report | Genworth." *Genworth*, www.genworth.com/aging-and-you/finances/cost-of-care.html. Accessed 12 July 2020.

27. Ibid.

28. "How Much Care Will You Need? - Long-Term Care Information." *LongTermCare.Gov*, longtermcare.acl.gov/the-basics/how-much-care-will-you-need.html. Accessed 12 July 2020.

29. RegisteredNursing.org Staff Writers. "Healthcare Costs & Spend: Rising by Age, Gender, and Race || RegisteredNursing.Org." *Registered Nursing*, 8 Jan. 2020, www.registerednursing.org/healthcare-costs-by-age.

30. "Find out Which States Have an Inheritance Tax with This Helpful Chart." *The Balance*, www.thebalance.com/state-inheritance-tax-chart-3505460. Accessed 12 July 2020.

31. Brian, Anderson. "Technology Changing the Way People Age: GRPAA Finnovation Conference." *401kspecialistmag.Com*, 4 Oct. 2019, 401kspecialist-mag.com/technology-changing-the-way-people-age-grp-finnovation-conference.

32 Best Places To Retire In 2019. (n.d.). Retrieved July 29, 2020, from https://www.forbes.com/best-places-to-retire/

.